Finding Conviction in the Cross

*Growing in our commitment to God,
through our knowledge of Him*

Michael Rowand

Table of Contents

Preface

At the time of writing this book I have lived in the southern United States the majority of my life. In that time I've seen a number of people who have a professing faith in Christ, but there are few who back that up. It's a superficial, cheap faith. I guess even worse than that, often it is fake. Those who claim to have a faith in Christ may worship him on Sunday morning but curse His name or use it in vain the other days of the week. This is not the way Christians are supposed to live. Christians should bear the image of Christ. They are supposed to be Christ-like. It seems the further we go down the time continuum, the further away from Christ we become both in time and in practice.

About a year ago, I was meeting with a friend who had made the same observations I had. He challenged me to write a book to show how one can go from a professing Christian to a mature Christian, who is firm in the faith. Little did he know, I had already given the idea some thought. After our conversation I knew I had to do something.

The church needs stronger Christians. We know that any group is only as strong as its weakest member. In the church we have a large number of weak members. If we want to witness to the 21st-century world and beyond, we need to be ready to pick up our weak members. Paul wrote about this in Galatians, *"Bear one another's burdens, and so fulfill the law of Christ."* Helping the weaker members grow will cause the church to be stronger. We need to move from fake faith to a strong, obedient, and active faith.

This book will not contain any excuses. Growing in Christ is a lifelong venture. It is the most challenging and demanding way to live your life. There will be sacrifices and there will be times that you do things that you wouldn't naturally do. However, we'll understand by the end of this book that it is worth more than anything this world has to offer. It is the highest goal of humanity: to serve God and to love him with all of our might. While that may be difficult, it is the created purpose we have been given. God has equipped us in such a way that we will be able to accomplish this task. In addition to that, God enables us to daily follow him. He has given us the tools necessary for following Him in this life. You can become mature in Christ. But, it will not just take place by the circumstances of your life, it is a choice to follow God.

Multiple times in Scripture God presented His people with a choice. Will they serve Him, or are they going to do their own thing? Growth is no different. If we want to become a mature Christian, one who follows Christ wherever he leads, we will have to make the choice to do so. From there we will make daily decisions that align our life with God's will, which changes us from the inside out. God will be working on our hearts through His word, and the discipline that we show in following Him.

Christians are called to exercise intense self-control. At the very heart of our faith is a desire to become like someone else, namely Christ himself. To accomplish that we must wrestle ourselves into submission and change who we are so that we become like Jesus. This is something we cannot do on our own; this transformation is a gift from God. The very fact that we are able to accomplish this is a gift of grace. It is grace and mercy given to us only by our Creator.

I want to share something else with you before we begin the main part of this book. A huge motivation I have in sharing these things with you is the fact that God offers us something. This gift is something that you have to experience. It is the gift that Jesus talks about in John 10. Jesus said that there were thieves that came to kill, steal, and destroy, but he said he came so that we might have life and have it abundantly. In Christ we find abundant life and that is the life I cannot explain. There is peace, joy, and security like nothing I've ever known. I used to think long and hard about what I can do to defend myself and my reputation. Now I worry so much less. I find the words of Jesus comforting. He commands his disciples not to worry about tomorrow's troubles, yet we spend so much of our time worrying about things that never end up happening. In Christ, our worries fade away. Those fears and concerns turn into faith. In Christ there is abundant life, with peace that surpasses all understanding. Within the word of God we find the keys to success. This book is an attempt to put those keys in one place, not that there is any way to contain all of Scripture or to oversimplify it. I plan to show you, through the scriptures, how to find life in Christ. This is not some cheap substitute for the good life. This is real, abundant life from God.

I hope you are ready for the ride, as we explore what it takes to grow in Christ. In so doing we will find conviction in the cross. Our conviction will propel us forward into growth that we have never experienced before. These deeply held beliefs will change our thinking, our actions, and our desires.

Throughout this book, I cite authors that wrote about concepts or ideas that support Biblical truths. Those inclusions in this book do not imply I agree with their beliefs or views on every doctrinal issue.

In Him,

Michael

Chapter 1

Power

"You don't have to be great to start, but you have to start to be great."
—Zig Ziglar

When are you going to start to be great? I cannot tell you how many times someone has told me "I can't do that" or "I'm not good enough to achieve that." I don't know exactly why it is, but it is true—we reserve greatness for a select few. Only people who are born with superhuman size, intelligence, or ability are allowed to be great. We might think there is no way that we can do anything special, because we were born into the wrong family, we don't have enough money, or we don't have the time to be great. We buy into a lie every time we think those things. Every time we believe that greatness is kept aside for a small group of people, we sell ourselves short; even worse, we sell God short. No one that achieved greatness started there. They had to start to be great.

You can become great! You can be a mature Christian. You have the opportunity to transform into a spiritual giant. You need to realize that God can use you to do great things. There are people who were worse off than you that achieved greatness in the name of Christ. God used liars, murderers, and opponents of His to accomplish great things. They led the people of God to new heights and completed God's will. Greatness, that will last, is achievement that God brings about through us. Doesn't this mean that you have the potential to serve God in a way that is far beyond how you are serving Him now?

Potential is a scary concept to think about, because with potential comes the opportunity not to reach it. Brian Houston is confident that he has figured out the reason we do not always reach our potential. *"So much potential perishes because of the lack of an audacious dream."*[1] I am confident that you have the potential for great things in the name of Christ. Are you dreaming big enough? For some, greatness would involve overcoming a sin that has plagued them their whole life. For others, it could mean studying the Bible with someone for the first time and seeing them come to Christ. It may be that greatness for you would be housing foster children or adopting a child. Are you dreaming about what you can do for the cause of Christ?

You may be thinking, "How is he so confident?" or "You have too much faith in me." The answer to those statements is not found in who you are. I am more than confident in you, because of the mighty power of God. God has empowered Christians to change the world. We can make a difference that can be felt around the globe. I would argue that Christians should be the most optimistic and hopeful people there are.

Before you accuse me of being too optimistic, let us look into the Bible for answers. Following the resurrection of Jesus and the establishment of the church, Christians faced intense persecution from the Jews. In one particular instance, jealousy led the high priest to have Jesus' apostles arrested. In the middle of the night an angel of the Lord freed them from prison. They went back to preaching and teaching the message of Jesus in the temple. The Jewish leaders were stunned when the apostles escaped from prison. They brought them again before the council and the high priest to question them. The Jewish leaders commanded the apostles not to teach in the name of Jesus. Of course, they objected because the apostles knew they needed to serve God above any man.

Peter, and the apostles, spoke to them about what they had done to Jesus. When the Jewish leaders heard these accusations, they became angry. They were ready to kill the apostles. A Pharisee, named Gamaliel, sent out the apostles so that he could speak freely with the rest of the council. Essentially, Gamaliel told them that they needed to be careful concerning the apostles. He pointed out the fact that if the Christians were not from God, then they would fail. In fact, Gamaliel cited other groups that had risen up and fallen very quickly. In each of those instances, men were at the forefront of the insurrections. After talk about these other false movements, he said,

Acts 5:38-39
"'So in the present case I tell you, keep away from these men and let them alone, for if this plan or this undertaking is of man, it will fail; but if it is of God, you will not be able to overthrow them. You might even be found opposing God!' So they took his advice."

God Is On Our Side

The simple, yet profound, fact that God is on our side should make all the difference. We have every reason for optimism and hope. You should have the confidence to dream big when it comes to how God can use you. Paul clearly says in Romans 8:31, *"If God is for us, who can be against us?"* The Church should be an unstoppable force in our communities. We should teach the lost about Jesus, help those in need, and care for other Christians. Simply put, the Church should make a difference in the world. The Church should succeed in what it does. Christians should be growing.

Why is it that so many of our churches are in decline in America? If God were on our side wouldn't we have unstoppable power? Is it possible that we have left God's side? I think Gamaliel would say that that is a distinct possibility.

After all, isn't this Creator God that we're talking about? He is self-described as the Almighty. How could a plan of His fail? It is obvious that God's plan would never fail. The issue is in our application of God's plan. Whenever there is consistent failure, it is not because of God. There is a lack of trust and commitment from His people. When there is a long period of decline, it is not God's fault. We need Him at the center of our plans, hopes, and dreams. His promises of His presence should remain at the forefront of our minds. The Church needs to remember all that God has promised. I can remember my dad saying in a sermon of his, *"We need to be standing on the promises, instead of sitting on the premises."* God's promises of strength, peace, and joy for the Church are just as powerful today as they were nearly two millennia ago.

In all of this, we must first recognize that we need God to be effective in impacting this lost and dying world. All of the authority and power is from God, which He gave to Jesus. Jesus, in turn, gave authority to the apostles when he sent them out on the great commission. The apostles gave that authority to the leaders of the churches. Paul specifically told Timothy in 2 Timothy 2:2, *"what you have heard from me in the presence of many witnesses entrust to faithful men, who will be able to teach others also."* The Epistles, that make up over half of the New Testament, are our evidence that the apostles constantly taught other church leaders. These lessons have been handed down to us through the ages. It is an act of God that we still have the Scriptures today in the form that they're in. We can find a direct connection to God's will through the Bible.

In the Bible we read about incredible things that God did through the Church. Very much like the words of Gamaliel, a concept of power is evident throughout the rest of the New Testament. Their message was incredibly simple—Jesus is the Christ. Jesus is the answer to the problem of sin in the world. There is no other name that saves other than Jesus.

Have you ever lost power in your house? It can be devastating in extreme conditions. Recently, my family experienced a similar phenomenon. We thought we had a reliable unit, but our heat suddenly stopped working. It baffled us. After a few hours we noticed our stove was reading an error message, and our lights were dim. We were experiencing a brownout. A brownout is when you have power but it is not at full strength. The power lines are damaged or disconnected, restricting your power. We can experience brownout as it relates to God. If we aren't connected fully and consistently to God, we will not fully experience all God has in store for us. Go back and look at Acts 5 with me. *"And every day, in the temple and from house to house, they did not cease teaching and preaching that the Christ is Jesus" (Acts 5:42).* They were talking about Jesus every day in the temple and in their homes.

If you are struggling in your faith, look first at your habits. Are you in the word of God daily? Do you pray consistently? When was the last time you were around other people who wanted to go to Heaven as badly as you do? We must fully connect to the power of God to experience the immensity of His power. Greatness in our lives will be based on whether or not God is working through us. The difference between strong Christians and every one else is how much they rely on God. An excellent example of this concept is Moses.

Example Of Moses

If we go back toward the beginning of our Bibles we find the book of Exodus. It depicts the exit of God's people from Egypt, where they were slaves. The Israelites grew so mighty that Pharaoh feared them. Out of fear, Pharaoh even decided to kill the newborn boys to limit their growth. One of the boys born during this time was named Moses. His parents protected him by putting him in a boat in the Nile River. By an act of God, Pharaoh's daughter found the boy in the river. Pharaoh's daughter commanded Moses' sister to find a nurse for the child. Moses mother, Jochebed, raised her child until he was weaned. From there, Moses was raised in the house of Pharaoh which meant that he learned about the customs and religions of the Egyptians. While he was out with the people one day, he observed an Egyptian beating a Hebrew. Moses struck and killed the Egyptian. As you can imagine, it wasn't very long before Pharaoh found out. Moses fled to the land of Midian where he found favor in the sight of the priest of Midian, Jethro.

One day when Moses was tending the flock in Midian, he saw something strange. A bush was burning, but it was not consumed. From the bush, the angel of the Lord appeared to him and spoke to him. God told Moses that he had seen the affliction of His people in Egypt. God said He would deliver them from the hand of the Egyptians. I have to think this would have excited Moses. His people would finally be free. God even promised that he was going to take them to a prosperous land, flowing with milk and honey. At the end of the promises God gave, He said that He was going to use Moses to bring his people out of Egypt. Moses' excitement turned to fear in the blink of an eye.

Moses had four main excuses for why he couldn't go back to Egypt.

1. He didn't think he was good enough.
2. He didn't think the people would know who God was.
3. He didn't think they would believe him and listen to him.
4. He didn't think he could speak well enough.

At the end of his excuses, Moses told God that it would be better for Him to send someone else. Benjamin Franklin described people like Moses when he said, *"He that is good for making excuses is seldom good for anything else."* You might be thinking to yourself, "How is it that God can use this man?" He doesn't even want to go. He doesn't have any confidence in himself. Moses was discouraged and lacked self-esteem.

You may feel like Moses today. You might think you are not very special. You may think that you don't really have any skills that could be used by God. Perhaps you think somebody else would do a better job than you would. It would be better for God to use someone else. I'm here to tell you that that is not the case. It's just not true. You can be great! God can use you no matter how inadequate you think you are. You see, God responded to every objection that Moses came up with. God made it possible for Moses to confront Pharaoh in Egypt. Moses's problem was that he relied only on himself for what needed to be done. When we focus on how good we are, we aren't going to get very far in this life. Instead of focusing on ourselves, we must focus on God. He is the Almighty. He is the One who empowers the church. He makes all the difference. God makes the impossible happen.

Thankfully, Moses was willing to go to Pharaoh. God twisted his arm just hard enough to get him to go to Egypt. After 10 plagues, Pharaoh finally let the Israelites go. God led the Israelites by a pillar of cloud and a pillar of fire into the wilderness. They came to the shores of the Red Sea and noticed that the Egyptian army had been following them. Pharaoh had changed his mind. The Egyptians were in 600 chariots coming with the force of their army. On the other hand, the Israelites had, most likely, between two and three million people. They were not able to move very quickly. If you've ever been to a sporting event, concert, or fair you realize that masses of people move very slowly. On top of all of that, they're stuck against the Red Sea. They had nowhere to go and nowhere to hide from the Egyptians. The people cry out to Moses and complain. They wished they had never left Egypt. Even though they were slaves they were living, or so they thought. It was at this moment, Moses emerged as the true leader of the people of Israel.

Exodus 14:13-14
"And Moses said to the people, 'Fear not, stand firm, and see the salvation of the Lord, which he will work for you today. For the Egyptians whom you see today, you shall never see again. The Lord will fight for you, and you have only to be silent.'"

Moses ultimately figured it out. He needed to trust God more than he relied on himself. In a situation where there seemed to be no way out, Moses pointed the Israelites to God. There are a few lessons that we should take from this passage.

First and foremost, God can do things that are beyond our comprehension. C. S. Lewis wrote in *Mere Christianity*, "To what will you look for help if you will not look to that which is stronger than yourself?"[2] I am thankful that God can do things far beyond my

11

scope of understanding. Time and time again, God did things in the Bible that blew people's minds. Obviously, the Israelites did not see this coming. They would not have complained about their situation if they had known what God was about to do. They walked through the Red Sea on dry ground and the water was a wall to them on the right hand and the left. The parting of the Red Sea is one of the most iconic miracles in all of the Scriptures. Moses knew that God would care for His people. God delivered the Israelites by doing something beyond their comprehension.

Second, we learn from Moses that leadership is about showing others the way to God. Before God called him, Moses did not seem to be all that special. Moses became special when he directed others to trust in God. Leaders must develop faith in other people. When the going gets tough, God's people trust Him more deeply. If Moses had given into fear and complained like the rest of the people, the result would have been different. Of course Moses knew how small the odds were. Of course Moses didn't exactly know how God was going to fight for them, but he knew that He would. Have faith in what God can do and encourage others to do so as well.

Lastly, we should recognize that we shouldn't be afraid. There are so many decisions made out of fear. Fear can control us and keep us from reaching our potential. This will not be all that is said in this book about fear, but it needs to be mentioned here. Moses urged the Israelites not to be afraid. He knew that God was going to fight for them. As I have already mentioned, *"If God is for us, who can be against us?" (Romans 8:31b)* If God is on our side, we don't have to let fear get us down.

From Moses' life we learn that it isn't about the vessel. God can use you. God caused Moses to grow and he became one of the

most influential men in all of human history. The power lies with
God. We need to submit to Him so that He can use us.

You may be asking, "How can I tap in to this power of
God?" The answer is threefold. In order to access the power of God
a Christian must be devoted to prayer, sacrifice, and service. J.
Hudson Taylor, who was a missionary to China, once said, *"When
God's work is done in God's way for God's glory, it will never lack God's
supply."* We cannot haphazardly be a Christian. We must serve God
in His way in order to receive His supplies. There will be an
emphasis on learning later in the book, but even learning has its
limitations. Knowledge for the sake of having knowledge leads to
arrogance. Prayer, sacrifice, and service give God the glory in
everything, which is the aim of our lives.

Prayer

*"Would you say that prayer plays any meaningful role in the life of your
church? If prayer isn't vital for your church, then your church isn't vital.
This statement may be bold, but I believe it's true. If you can accomplish
your church's mission without daily, passionate prayer, then your mission
is insufficient and your church is irrelevant." —Francis Chan[3]*

Based upon Chan's emphasis on prayer, would your church
be considered alive or dead? Would you consider prayer a
meaningful part of your life? When you face difficulty where do
you turn? When times are really good what is your first response?

Whenever a small child stumbles and falls, they get up and
run to their parents. They hide their face in their parent's knee.
Mom and Dad make them feel safe and comfortable. The child's
parents love them in such a way that gives them a sense of
protection. The opposite circumstances end with similar results.

When they color a picture, they run to Mom and Dad, proud of what they have colored. They're excited to show their parents what they have been working on.

In 1 John 3:1 we read, *"See what kind of love the Father has given to us, that we should be called children of God; and so we are."* God is not called 'Father' very much in the Old Testament. According to Baker's Evangelical Dictionary of Biblical Theology, He is only referred to as a Father fifteen times in the entire Old Testament. On the other hand, in the New Testament He is called Father consistently. *"The teaching of the Fatherhood of God takes a decided turn with Jesus, for 'Father' was his favorite term for addressing God. It appears on his lips some sixty-five times in the Synoptic Gospels and over one hundred times in John."*[4] Jesus coming to this earth began a new era of intimacy with God, the Father.

After all, it is because of Jesus that we have been welcomed into the family of God. This sort of relationship has its perks. One of those is our connection with God, through prayer. I think the reason Chan is so adamant about prayer is because it shows whether or not we depend on God. How much do we take to the Lord in prayer? If it's abundantly clear that we need God, shouldn't we be taking everything to God in prayer? If God is our Father, shouldn't we carry our cares, our concerns, and our difficulties to Him? If God is our Father, shouldn't we carry our successes and our victories to Him? We would be disappointed if our children never talked to us. How do you suppose God feels when He knows that He has what it takes to help us but we don't reach out to Him?

"I cannot imagine any one of you tantalizing your child by exciting in him a desire that you did not intend to gratify. It were a very ungenerous thing to offer alms to the poor, and then when they hold out their hand for it, to mock their poverty with a denial. It were a cruel addition to the

*miseries of the sick if they were taken to the hospital and there left to die
untended and uncared for. Where God leads you to pray, He means you to
receive."-Charles Spurgeon*

Time and time again the Bible speaks to the importance of
prayer. Why would God lead the writers to write so much about
something that was empty? Spurgeon hit the nail on the head. God
has intentions to bless us richly. Prayer needs to be at the center of
our life. We have already observed that God is able to make
amazing things happen in your life. Prayer is one of the ways we
access that power.

Paul closed a prayer of his with some of the greatest words
ever penned.

Ephesians 3:20-21
*Now to him who is able to do far more abundantly than all that we ask or
think, according to the power at work within us, to him be glory in the
church and in Christ Jesus throughout all generations, forever and ever.
Amen.*

He made it known that God is able to do immeasurably and
abundantly more than all we can ask or imagine. You cannot
imagine what God can do through your life. Even in your wildest
dreams you could not understand what God could do with you.
You could plan what you want your life to look like in five years,
then crumple that up. You can throw your plans away, because God
could make them tremble before what He actually has in mind for
you.

Future blessings are from a Being who calls Himself our
Father. He made the way possible to be with Him. This Father loves
us so much that He gave his only Son for us. God wants to equip

you to do great things in His service. We must pray for His blessings. There are blessings and growth that only He could provide. Logically, you must pray to someone stronger than you. When we pray, we give credit and honor to God, because we know He is stronger than us. He's way stronger. It's not even a contest. Prayer reveals our heart. Do we trust in God's power or our own? If we want to tap in to God's never ending power, we must be committed to prayer.

In everything, Jesus is our example. We are called Christians, after all. If prayer is valuable, we would expect to see Jesus committing time to pray. A brief look at the Gospels reveals a clear trend. Jesus was extremely committed to times of prayer. There were actually times that Jesus would stop doing other good things in order to go off to a desolate place to pray (Luke 5:15-16). Jesus is God in the flesh. He still needed spend time talking to God, his Father. The night before he died he prayed so fervently that he sweat drops of blood (Luke 22:44). Prayer was valuable to him because it connected him to God. Likewise, we must remain connected to Him. Our power comes from God, the Almighty. If Jesus felt compelled to pray, we surely need to!

Sacrifice

In much of the world, it's citizens are conditioned to look out for themselves. There is a striving to please number one—self. In fact, from a very young age, children are taught that they are the center of attention. With marketing and commercials the consumer is the most important person in the world. This attitude carries over into how we view the church. We may look for a church that pleases our needs and doesn't really consider the needs of others. The words of John F. Kennedy ring true all these years later, when he said, *"Ask not what your country can do for you – ask what you can do for your country,"*[5] The church should not be a place of entertainment, rather a place of sacrifice and service. Jesus spoke consistently about the sacrifices that Christians would have to make. Some of them would be big and some of them small. Our very lives are now viewed as a living sacrifice to God.

The early church is an excellent example of this sort of sacrifice. They were selling their possessions and giving to those who had need. Before the stoning of Stephen all of the Christians were living in Jerusalem. There were some who had traveled far distances from their homes to worship in Jerusalem when they were converted to Christ. Some new Christians had no resources or place to stay, so other Christians had to take care of their needs. The Christians with money shared everything, and not one thing was their own.

If we want to harness the power of the early church, we will be committed to the same things to which they were committed. Their example continues to shine as a light in the darkness to us. Do we model this in any way, shape, or form? Are our churches teaching sacrifice the way the early church did?

Jesus confronted this very issue head-on because he knew mankind's tendency to desire wealth. A rich man came to Jesus and asked him what he needed to do to inherit eternal life. He explained that he had kept all the commandments from his childhood. The rich man hadn't murdered anybody, he hadn't stolen from anybody, and he hadn't taken another man's wife. However, Jesus told him that he still lacked something. He told him, *"Sell what you possess and give to the poor, and you will have treasure in heaven; and come, follow me"* (Matthew 19:21b). As you might expect, this disturbed the rich man. The Bible described the encounter as bothersome to him, because he had great possessions.

Jesus sensed that the rich man would be unwilling to give up his stuff. Even though it was uncomfortable, Jesus called this man to sacrifice what he valued most.

How do you define yourself? It's likely that your first explanations are based on your career, or where you live, or your hobbies. While those are all wonderful things and they are descriptions of you, they aren't who you are. If you claim to have an identity in Christ, those other titles shouldn't be permanent. As Christians, we should hold on to things in this life lightly. We hold firmly to the cross of Christ, since the cross is where we see sacrifice embodied.

There is no question that Jesus' followers are called to sacrifice. Sacrifice may take any number of forms. We should be asking ourselves the question, "What can I do for the church?" The early church was first focused on the mission. They knew that they needed to reach as many people as possible. They were concerned with other people, rather than themselves. Sacrifice came naturally to them because they were thinking about others.

The power of God is wonderful, but He uses willing vessels. If you are so full of yourself, there will be no room for God's purposes. If we are so busy with our own plans and objectives, God will find no place in our hearts. The rich man that came to Jesus was incorrect. He had not kept the commandments from his early days, because it appears that he had broken the first commandment, which is to put no other gods before Almighty God. He had placed his possessions, and perhaps his social status, ahead of service to God. It seems like he tried to serve God and money. These two goals compete with one another and are unable to be harmonized. Jesus taught that we cannot serve God and money.

A parable comes to my mind that explains the need for sacrifice—the parable of the hidden treasure (Matthew 13:44). A man finds a treasure in a field. He determines that the treasure is worth more than what he owned. He sold all that he had in order to buy the field. He knew that the sum total of his possessions was not as valuable as what he had found. This parable instructs us in the way of the kingdom of God. A relationship with God is worth more than the sum total of your life. There is nothing that you own that is more valuable than the kingdom of God. When we understand how great and majestic the opportunity is before us, we will be willing to give whatever it takes to obtain it. I'm here to tell you that the life God offers is worth more than your job, than your possessions, and your hobbies.

It is attractive to think that more money or more stuff will reduce stress but the statistics show the opposite. In 2018, LinkedIn learning conducted a study on the amount of stress different jobs had. They found, *"47 percent of people making $35,000-to-$50,000 a year said they were stressed at work. Conversely, 68 percent of people making more than $200,000+ annually said they were stressed at work."*[6] There happened to be more stress with higher paying jobs than with jobs with less pay. This study shows money does not buy happiness. It cannot give you peace or joy. Money can't show you love or friendship. It is the wrong place to look for those things. There is a restlessness in your soul that was placed there by God and one that can only be filled with Him. Augustine of Africa echoed this sentiment, *"O God! Thou hast made us for Thyself and our souls are restless, searching, 'till they find their rest in Thee."* We will only find rest when we find it in God. God called His people to a life of sacrifice, which leads to eternal life.

It is significant that Jesus did not teach something that he was unwilling to follow through with himself. He is the template of sacrifice. He left the very throne room of God, was born into a poor family, served in ministry with no home to speak of, and he was killed in the most dishonorable way of that time. He allowed this mistreatment. When they were trying to arrest him, he claimed that he could have called legions of angels to defend him. The armies of heaven were at his disposal, but he was willing to be spit upon, to be harassed, to be beaten, and to be crucified.

Jesus sacrificed his life because he loved you. I don't know about you, but when I consider what Christ did for me, I can't help but feel a desire to sacrifice for him. That sacrifice may be my time, my energy, and my pride. I strive to be ready to sacrifice anything for his cause. I want to be ready to be homeless and hated for the sake of the Gospel. I want to be ready to be persecuted. I know that whatever might happen to me happened to Christ first. God was able to resurrect Jesus and I know that that same Spirit is ready to resurrect me.

God will use those who are humble and willing to sacrifice. If we are being used by God, His power will be the wind in our sails. There will not be a sacrifice of any kind that will go unnoticed. With His power, nothing is impossible.

Service

"Everybody can be great...because anybody can serve. You don't have to have a college degree to serve. You don't have to make your subject and verb agree to serve. You only need a heart full of grace. A soul generated by love." —Martin Luther King Jr.

The secret to greatness is not found in success or fame. Greatness is found in what we are doing for God and for others. Martin Luther King Jr. shed light on this when he said that we didn't need to be anything special to serve. If you have a love for God and others, you already have the tools to be great. If it is that simple, why aren't more of us known for service? Is that why a lot of Christians feel defeated or lost? If we recommitted to service, perhaps we would see revival.

If we want to have the power of God, we will be committed to prayer, sacrifice and service. Sacrifice and service are two sides of a coin. Sacrifice involves the giving up of things that keep us from serving God; whereas, service is a positive act for another entity. The call of Christ demands a willingness to give up and a desire to do for others.

The real key to sacrifice and service is humility. Christians are humbled because of what Christ did for them. Jesus called his disciples to serve others. There was actually an instance in which the disciples were fighting for dominance. We may think the apostles were perfect, never fighting amongst themselves; however, that is definitely not the case. Jesus responded by saying, *"If anyone would be first, he must be last of all and servant of all"* (Mark 9:35). Again, the key to greatness is found in how often we serve. Not only that, but it is about how we view ourselves. We have a tendency to think we are better than our peers. Jesus said the last will be first. Christians must consider other people, no matter who they are, as more important than themselves. Martin Luther King Jr. had mastered one of Jesus' core teachings. Humility compels us into service, which leads to greatness.

The first century Church was blessed with good leadership. Their actions were modeled after the Lord, which led them into success. One of the best things they did was carry on the commitment to service. Paul, Timothy, James, Peter, Jude, and John all introduce themselves at the beginning of letters as servants. These men cast out demons and healed the sick. They started church after church across the known world. It would have been a temptation to become conceited and arrogant. Their diligence in service is a lesson on how important it should be to us. The apostle Paul gave us some insight into the process of making a difference.

1 Corinthians 3:5-7
What then is Apollos? What is Paul? Servants through whom you believed, as the Lord assigned to each. I planted, Apollos watered, but God gave the growth. So neither he who plants nor he who waters is anything, but only God who gives the growth.

Both Apollos and Paul had essential roles in sharing the Gospel message, one was the initial worker and the other helped carry it along. Neither was responsible for the good that happened. It is God who gives the growth. He made it clear. Christians are servants that are a part of the process of sharing the Good News, but it is ultimately God who deserves the credit. Did you notice His role in all of this? God blesses and causes things to grow.

Power From God

Do you want to accomplish great things? Submit to the will of God, becoming a servant in His vineyard. Do something in His name. Whenever we yield to God, through obedience, amazing things will happen. There will be other people around us who will be impacted. Whenever an entire church submits to God, an entire community can be changed. In the first century, we see that exact thing happening.

Paul and Silas were traveling and sharing the Gospel as they went. They would reason with the Jews in the synagogue. There were Jews who became Christians, but there were others who began to be jealous. They formed a mob that attacked some Christians there. Their first words are compelling, *"These men who have turned the world upside down have come here also, and Jason has received them, and they are all acting against the decrees of Caesar, saying that there is another King, Jesus" (Acts 17:6b-7).* The Christians in Thessalonica were making a difference that was felt by others. The impact on their community was real and palpable. Why did the Jews say that the Christians had turned the world upside down? The answer begins with their King, Jesus.

Jesus came to this earth according to the purpose of God. He came to unite mankind with God. Our sins are like the Colorado River that tears open the Grand Canyon. There was a need for a sacrifice that would repair the bond that sin tore apart. Jesus is the sacrifice that reunited mankind with the perfect God. Paul and Silas were proclaiming that Jesus was the Christ, the Anointed One. The Jews did not recognize him as the Savior. Their personal bias and selfishness kept them from seeing who Jesus truly was. On the other hand, the Christians that followed Paul and Silas were submitting to Christ as their King. The Kingship of Christ changed their lives. They were no longer practicing Jews; instead, they followed the teachings of Jesus.

When Christ is our King, our world is turned upside down. Jesus called his disciples to a life of self-denial and holiness. We are no longer living for ourselves; we are living to please God. I think the apostle Paul said it best in Acts 20:24, *"But I do not account my life of any value nor as precious to myself, if only I may finish my course and the ministry that I received from the Lord Jesus, to testify to the gospel of the grace of God."* Our entire purpose is wrapped up in the purposes of God.

If the Church submits to God, serves Him, and considers their life as of little value, the world will be turned upside down.

God's power would flow freely through us. If you commit to those things, His power will stream through your life. You will be impacting the lost. You will be healing broken bonds in your relationships. You will be great.

Chapter 2

Learn

"Being ignorant is not so much a shame, as being unwilling to learn."
—*Benjamin Franklin*

From the time we are born, our life is characterized by learning. You have to learn to talk, walk, work, and eat cookies. We come in to this world with a relatively blank slate that we have to fill with the wonders this world has to offer. A baby is quick to seek what pleases them and they will let you know about it, loudly.

I don't really know what it is or when it takes place, but there comes a point when we feel like we have arrived. There is a temptation to give up on the lifelong pursuit of knowledge. The Devil is excellent at deceiving men and women to give up on learning. Whether its pride or indifference, learning gets put in the backseat for other seemingly more important activities. Ironically, the more information we have in our hands because of our technology, the less we know. Dr. Tomas Chamorro-Premuzic said this in an article for *Psychology Today*, *"Unsurprisingly, with all the knowledge of the world being now outsourced, crowdsourced, and cloudsourced, the individual storage of information is minimal (at least in comparison). Humans today are like most smartphones and tablets - their ability to solve problems depends not on the knowledge they can store but on their capacity to connect to a place where they can retrieve the answer to find a solution.*"[1] The amount we actually know has decreased because of how easily information can be accessed. While it is wonderful to know where things are, it is disturbing that modern society is growing less functional when there is no connectivity.

Benjamin Franklin recognized that knowledge wasn't as important as an eagerness to learn. If there is a desire to learn, any ignorance can be overcome, especially in this day and time. We do have access to limitless information that we can drink in. There is something here that is essential to the life of the Christian. Whether you realize it now or not, the Christian's identity is only found through learning. There is no alternate course.

Disciples

Followers of Jesus were characterized, in the New Testament, as disciples. The word is used over two hundred and fifty times in the Gospels and Acts.[2] According to *A Greek-English Lexicon of the New Testament*, the word that is translated 'disciple' has the primary meaning of *"one who engages in learning through instruction from another."*[3] Simply put, followers of Jesus were defined as learners. This makes good sense when we think of the twelve apostles. There had never been a teacher of Jesus' stature and there never will be. The apostles were his original disciples; they were in direct contact with the Lord.

Jesus having his own disciples was consistent with the practices of that day. The other rabbis would have disciples as well. Jesus criticized the early teachers for their arrogance, because they used their position to stroke their own ego. This disciple and teacher relationship would be the equivalent to a craftsman and their apprentice. A craftsman teaches an apprentice the skills they would need in order to be successful in their particular trade. The apprentice would develop into a professional themselves and they could eventually acquire new understudies of their own. Likewise, Jesus taught his disciples, who taught the following generation of disciples, who taught the following generation, and so on. Where did the disconnect take place? There are multitudes of 'Christians' who know nothing about the Bible nor the things of God. Where did our love for learning go? To where did the humility it takes to learn, from another, vanish? Members of the body of Christ must recover their desire to be a disciple, or student, of Jesus.

If Christians considered themselves as students of Jesus, no matter their age, our ignorance would disappear rather quickly. Our learning would become knowledge, which would speedily become conviction. Our convictions, the beliefs that we hold most dear to us, shape our behavior. If you want to have your life transformed by the power of Jesus, you will start with your mind. You will learn the teachings of Jesus and the apostles, and you will be remade from the inside out.

We have already considered the Almighty Power of God. He is able to bring about transformation that no other being can accomplish. Remember Moses' journey to great faith in God. No two ways about it, he was a coward and unmotivated. God changed his heart into that of a lion. Moses was a courageous, unstoppable leader of God's people. In the same way, God can change you. You may not know much right now; but you have to start somewhere. Don't let a lack of knowledge keep you from a deep relationship with God. Begin, today, to be a student of Jesus. As we will see from Scripture, seeing yourself as a disciple of Christ makes a huge difference.

Ephesians 4:17-19
Now this I say and testify in the Lord, that you must no longer walk as the Gentiles do, in the futility of their minds. They are darkened in their understanding, alienated from the life of God because of the ignorance that is in them, due to their hardness of heart. They have become callous and have given themselves up to sensuality, greedy to practice every kind of impurity.

Ignorance leads to wrongdoing. These verses, along with the next section of verses, juxtapose two groups of people. First, the Gentiles who did not know God. They were ignorant of the things of God and His purposes. Paul described them as futile in their minds and said their understanding was darkened. This ignorance gives way to a hardening of the heart or, perhaps, the hardness of the heart leads to ignorance. Either way, this group of people did not know God. In the passage, we see that this ignorance leads to every kind of impurity.

It starts in the mind. If someone does not know God, their actions will likely show that. If someone has a strong view of God, their actions will also show that. Our concept of God influences our way of life.

Existence Of God

Christians are in a tough spot right now, because atheism and agnosticism are on the rise. Immorality is becoming the norm, rather than the exception. Christians must first show that there is a God before they can teach unbelievers about morality. Christians are labeled as bigots because they are following a different standard from the rest of the world. If atheists believed in objective truth from an Almighty God, then Christians would be better understood. For many years, Christians have neglected to defend the position that there is a God; the general moral degradation has proven that.

You must first have a belief in God. If you don't know whether or not God exists, that mountain should be climbed first. You must believe that God exists before you can see the importance of Christ's teachings. If you do not know God, I would try to convince you that there is a God before I want to talk to you about morality and what God expects of you. Kyle Butt and Eric Lyons outline a number of logical proofs for the existence of God in their book, *Reasons To Believe*. Among the many proofs from their research, consider the fact that design demands a designer.[4] The universe is designed with specific dimensions that keep it from collapsing on itself. The human body is designed in such a way that it can repair itself and function properly on its own in most cases. Where do these designs come from? Logically, a carefully considered design demands a designer.

The fact that God exists changes reality. Life is no longer a result of improbable explosions or other evolutionary forces, but it is a gift from a wonderful, loving Creator. We should view our lives as a service or gift back to Him, in which we devote our existence to the One who made us. In Ephesians 4, the Gentiles did not know God and it affected their behavior. G. K. Chesterton knew this when he said, *"When men choose not to believe in God, they do not thereafter believe in nothing, they then become capable of believing in anything."* When there is no belief in God, all bets are off the table. I will concede that if there is no God, there is no need for harsh moral standards. Christians would be bigoted and wrong for forcing their way of life on others. The problem with this though, is there is a God and He is *alive*. The fact of God's existence changes everything. The appeal of Christians to bring others to God is not out of hate or anger; rather, it is out of love. We strive to love the way Christ loved us.

It all starts in the mind. The other nations, who did not know God, were living in sin because they did not know Him. Our lives are changed when we understand that God exists and that He rewards those who follow Him. He has standards of morality and lifestyle. God expects people to live in a certain way. He now orders our lives, but it's with our best interest in mind. God cares deeply for us. At every point, He has shown His love for us.

Ephesians 4:20-24
But that is not the way you learned Christ!—assuming that you have heard about him and were taught in him, as the truth is in Jesus, to put off your old self, which belongs to your former manner of life and is corrupt through deceitful desires, and to be renewed in the spirit of your minds, and to put on the new self, created after the likeness of God in true righteousness and holiness.

With the first word of verse twenty we see that there is a clear change of subject. The Ephesians were not committed to every kind of impurity. Instead, they were committed to following Christ. Notice all the words used to describe what it means to become a Christian: 'learned,' 'taught,' and 'renewed in the spirit of your minds'. These acts involve learning from Christ. A Christian is committed to learning what Christ was like, what he valued, and how he treated others. The aim is to conform to this image. When we know what Christ looked like, we can then incorporate that into our own lives. Our transformation is based on learning. We learn about the error of our old life, and see the blessings of the new life God has for us. There is hope and peace in Christ.

There is great value in learning what Christ taught. Read the Bible for yourself, and understand his teachings. Jesus was committed to speaking the truth, at all times. His teachings involve doing what is in the best interest of others, because he lived as a servant. Nowhere did he promote violence as the answer to personal matters. Instead, he preached turning the other cheek to the one who does evil to you. Jesus praised qualities and actions like love, purity, peacemaking, service, and humility. A thorough reading of the Gospels will reveal the teachings of Christ, which should transform our actions.

In the middle of all this we find an opportunity to be renewed in the spirit of our minds. HELPS Word studies, through Biblehub.com, provides some insight on the Greek verb here for renewed, *"Here believers are reminded of God's continuous offer to bring new strides in their sanctification through 'sanctified reasoning' – raising the meaning up to new levels of spiritual comprehension and reality."*[5] God is helping us along the way in our learning. He is able to offer deeper levels of knowledge to Christians, that we never thought possible. We will look further into the Spirit's role in all of this later, but the Spirit aides us in our understanding. God wants Christians to be diligent in their studies of Him.

Learning About Our Creator

"The Bible is not an end in itself, but a means to bring men to an intimate and satisfying knowledge of God, that they may enter into Him, that they may delight in His Presence, may taste and know the inner sweetness of the very God Himself in the core and center of their hearts." —A. W. Tozer[6]

31

Tozer unlocked the secret to Bible study. It is not that we need to memorize a book of facts and figures. It is not that we need to know a certain amount of the Bible to get into Heaven. The reason for the importance of Bible study is, we meet God through the Scriptures. We have an opportunity to meet God afresh each and every day. God reveals Himself to us through the written word. We don't have to guess or speculate about what He wants from us; we can read about how we come to an *"intimate and satisfying knowledge of God."*

The apostle Paul knew the importance of having a deep, individual connection to God. He prayed that the church at Ephesus would be strengthened with power, through God's Spirit, in their inner being in Ephesians 3:16. There is power in the Spirit of God. He also wanted them to improve their inner being. Do you ever pray for inner fortitude? Do you pray that your heart would be strengthened and your mind empowered? Donald Whitney, in his book *Spiritual Disciplines for the Christian Life*, said, *"Christians must realize that just as fire cannot blaze without fuel, so burning hearts are not kindled by brainless heads."*[7] We should be striving to grow in our minds and thoughts. Additionally, we need to pray to God for strength that only He can provide. There has to be reservoirs of power that only God can distribute; otherwise, why would Paul pray for it? As Christians, we should be looking to learn and grow into Christ. Peter wrote that we should grow in the grace and knowledge of our Lord Jesus Christ (2 Peter 3:18). We should pray for this daily, that our minds may grow like Christ's mind. Christians can be thankful that God aspires to help us develop in Him. God has put a burning desire in our hearts to worship Him, which He will help us quench.

Anyone with the ability to read or listen can learn about the One who made them, the One who loves them, and the One who

has made a way for eternal life. You are able to learn about the
Majestic One who sits on the throne. In the middle of the Bible
there is a book with Songs and Prayers to the Lord. Great
individuals of faith wrote the Psalms, where they poured out their
heart before God. Of all the things the Psalmists could pray and
sing about, they frequently chose learning and instruction. An
inspection of the Psalms leads us to the core of the importance of
learning.

Psalm 25:4
Make me to know your ways, O Lord;
teach me your paths.

Psalm 27:11
Teach me your way, O Lord,
and lead me on a level path
because of my enemies.

Psalm 86:11
Teach me your way, O Lord,
that I may walk in your truth;
unite my heart to fear your name.

Psalm 119:9-12
How can a young man keep his way pure?
By guarding it according to your word.
With my whole heart I seek you;
let me not wander from your commandments!
I have stored up your word in my heart,
that I might not sin against you.

Blessed are you, O Lord;
teach me your statutes!

Psalm 119:18
Open my eyes, that I may behold
wondrous things out of your law.

Psalm 143:10
Teach me to do your will,
for you are my God!
Let your good Spirit lead me
on level ground!

Psalm 119:135
Make your face shine upon your servant,
and teach me your statutes.

From each of these Psalms we see a desire to learn from God, which stems from an aspiration to serve God. There is a connection between learning and serving God. The Psalmists wanted to know the laws of God, so that they would not sin against God. None of us would admit a desire to sin against God, but it is tempting to put learning on the back burner. We learn from others, that a deep devotion to the Lord begins with learning His desire for us. Thankfully, there is always more to learn.

"Every time I walk to the Bible to study it, I feel like a man walking to the ocean with a teaspoon to dip it dry." —TB Larimore

We cannot ever know all there is to know. God is infinitely wiser than us. His word is complex, yet simple. It was never meant to be a textbook that was learned for the sake of having knowledge. The Bible is meant to change our lives. The words of God govern our conduct in this life. Christians are called to selflessness and a deep commitment to God, which manifests itself in learning. Our willingness to learn is a form of submission before God. We are living in the way that He prescribes. One reason that God's word feels like an ocean to be dipped dry, is its applicability. The Bible has an answer for every situation. From God's word we know how we should feel about the sanctity of life. The Bible taught us about dealing with those we don't see eye to eye with. We have the answer to the origin of the universe. God has blessed us with answers concerning these things, in the Bible.

As we have studied to this point, we can see that learning is of the utmost importance. A Christian should be learning so that he/she can know more about how God would want His people to live. Having an immense amount of knowledge can seem like a daunting task. Thankfully, God has laid out a way that we can receive all of His blessings.

Jesus was on this earth for a finite amount of time—approximately 33 years. While he was here, Jesus preached the message of the nearness of the kingdom and showed the love of God to the world. It would be tempting to think that it would have been better for Jesus to be a member of the early Church to guide it. Why did God not want Jesus to stay on the earth longer? First of all, he had to be the atoning sacrifice for the Church. The price of blood had to be paid for the establishment of the Church; there is no other way around it. The second reason for Jesus needing to leave the earth is found in the Gospel of John.

Learning From The Holy Spirit

John 16:7, 12-15
Nevertheless, I tell you the truth: it is to your advantage that I go away,
for if I do not go away, the Helper will not come to you. But if I go, I will
send him to you.

"I still have many things to say to you, but you cannot bear them now.
When the Spirit of truth comes, he will guide you into all the truth, for he
will not speak on his own authority, but whatever he hears he will speak,
and he will declare to you the things that are to come. He will glorify me,
for he will take what is mine and declare it to you. All that the Father has
is mine; therefore I said that he will take what is mine and declare it to
you."

The plan of God contained sending the Holy Spirit down to
mankind. Jesus explained to the apostles that it would be better for
them to have the Holy Spirit than to have him with them. The Spirit
led the apostles into all truth, and He gave them the words to say
before other people.

The Spirit of God being with the apostles was beneficial for a
number of reasons. As soon as the apostles had the Spirit, God
could always be with them instead of only the times they were in
the presence of Jesus. There are only so many people who can be
around Jesus at one time, due to physical limitations. In the Bible
we read that anyone who is baptized into Christ is given the gift of
the Holy Spirit. The Spirit dwells within believers. In the age of the
Church, believers can have God with them all the time. The Church
was able to go throughout much, if not all, of the known world
because of the Spirit of God. The church was able to accomplish
things it would not have been able to, if Jesus stayed on the earth.

Additionally, since the apostles had the Holy Spirit, they were able to perform miracles that no one else was able to do. The signs and wonders they did proved the message they carried with them. There was no written record of the importance of Jesus at this point. The Old Testament Scriptures were their only source of information, but it did not explain the Gospel the way the early Church needed it. The apostles provided further explanation, describing how the Christ was Jesus. He was the one that was prophesied about for centuries. Jesus was the one that they were looking for and the Holy Spirit allowed the apostles to make that message clear to the nations, through their miracles.

The third reason for the Holy Spirit coming to the apostles is they were able to write down what the Spirit communicated to them. This blessing is still benefiting Christians to this day. What the apostles wrote leads the church in every place that has a New Testament in that respective language. Peter explained the importance of divine inspiration in his second letter that he wrote.

2 Peter 1:16-21
For we did not follow cleverly devised myths when we made known to you the power and coming of our Lord Jesus Christ, but we were eyewitnesses of his majesty. For when he received honor and glory from God the Father, and the voice was borne to him by the Majestic Glory, "This is my beloved Son, with whom I am well pleased," we ourselves heard this very voice borne from heaven, for we were with him on the holy mountain. And we have the prophetic word more fully confirmed, to which you will do well to pay attention as to a lamp shining in a dark place, until the day dawns and the morning star rises in your hearts, knowing this first of all, that no prophecy of Scripture comes from someone's own interpretation. For no prophecy was ever produced by the will of man, but men spoke from God as they were carried along by the Holy Spirit.

There will always be those who oppose God's purposes. Today, there are still groups who oppose the word of God. I'm sure in Peter's day there were objectors, who questioned the New Testament authors. He points out though that it was not a cleverly devised myth, because he was there. Like many of the other authors, Peter was writing the things that he had intimate knowledge about. He was present when the Lord was transformed, and Moses and Elijah appeared. He didn't have to quote or cite another source. He was the source. In our courts today, eyewitness testimony is still highly valued. If someone says they saw something, we usually believe what they say. We may look for someone to corroborate their story, but if they're a trustworthy person we believe their testimony. In this case, we have the testimony of what Peter saw. His testimony that Jesus is the Christ, the Son of the living God, is in harmony with the other New Testament authors. If the story of Jesus along with the subsequent writings was a lie, there would be plenty of people who could have stood up and refuted what the apostles wrote. No such record exists.

Beyond the apostles and other writers agreeing with one another, it should be noted that the entire Bible is written by around 40 people over a span of some 1,500 years. Their location covers a vast area as well. How can all these men share stories that line up with one another? They came from all walks of life: shepherds, fisherman, kings, prophets, warriors, and even a tax collector. It would take an act of God for all of those people to write a book that agrees with itself on specific moral doctrines and events. Peter is trying to tell his audience that the words that have been written are important. Actually, they are life-changing because they are the words of God. The inspiration of the apostles comes directly from the Holy Spirit. He led them to write what they wrote.

Since the Holy Spirit led the apostles to write the New Testament, it is a lamp shining in a dark place. Like the psalmist before, Peter knew how important it was to know the word of God. It is a map that guides us.

"Sink the Bible to the bottom of the ocean, and still man's obligations to God would be unchanged. He would have the same path to tread, only his lamp and guide would be gone; the same voyage to make, but his chart and compass would be overboard!" —Henry Ward Beecher

2 Timothy 3:16-17
All Scripture is breathed out by God and profitable for teaching, for reproof, for correction, and for training in righteousness, that the man of God may be complete, equipped for every good work.

The Scriptures, that we hold dear, are constantly equipping us for the work that God has laid out for His people. The words have eternal value since they come from the very breath of God. The Bible is allowing us to grow; God is teaching us through it. Without the word of God to guide us, we would be drifting along waiting for help. On the other hand, we have access to the word of God—which teaches us the way. The Bible is a direct result of the work of the Spirit. Paul even calls the Sword of the Spirit the word of God in the book of Ephesians. We have a direct link to God through the Bible. Consider the chain of authority: God created the universe by the words of His mouth, the Word became flesh and dwelt among us, the Spirit came to the apostles, and the apostles completed the writings for the Bible as we know it. We can trace the authority back to God through the Scriptures. Why wouldn't we

want to learn from the very word of God? Praise be to the Spirit
who makes this possible!

Committed To Learning

The church should champion learning and every member
should be involved in it. If you want to find conviction in the Cross
you must know the importance of the Cross. In the Scriptures, we
see the depth of God's love for us in Christ's sacrifice. Jesus is our
peace, our righteousness, the one who sanctifies us, the one who
purifies us, and our propitiation. His sacrifice means the world to
us. Actually, it should mean more than the world to us. It should be
the most valuable thing we have and experience. The more we
learn about Christ, the deeper our service should go.

Learning can take many shapes and sizes. A student of
Christ will be committed to his teachings. This means that he or she
will study the Bible continually. There are many apps and services
that offer a daily Bible verse which can kick-start a daily study.
There are countless blogs and recorded sermons on the internet. If
you are involved in a local church, I am sure that there are Bible
study groups that you can be a part of. If there are not, start your
own. Where I worship, there are many small Bible studies that go
on in people's homes in addition to congregational Bible studies. A
commitment to learning can come in many forms, but the
commitment must be there. Thankfully, God is there to help. He
blesses our efforts. You will never put more in than He will.
Studying God's word will multiply the blessings he gives to you.
There is renewal, peace, hope, and faith found in the Scriptures. We
are taught how to live, and that carries us from day to day. We meet
God in the scriptures which should motivate us to go back to them
each day.

In a large portion of the world, the Bible is readily available. A Barna Group Study in 2017 revealed that 87% of American households owned a Bible.[8] Not only that, but anyone with internet access has a limitless number of Bible resources in their own language. This sort of over-saturation can breed complacency. There is a temptation to view the word of God as commonplace or just another book. Consider one last passage of the New Testament about learning:

1 Peter 1:10-12
Concerning this salvation, the prophets who prophesied about the grace that was to be yours searched and inquired carefully, inquiring what person or time the Spirit of Christ in them was indicating when he predicted the sufferings of Christ and the subsequent glories. It was revealed to them that they were serving not themselves but you, in the things that have now been announced to you through those who preached the good news to you by the Holy Spirit sent from heaven, things into which angels long to look.

Before Jesus came, there was an anticipation for the Messiah. The Jewish people were waiting and longing for him to come save Israel from their troubles. The prophets of old didn't get to experience the wonders of the Christ. You do! Peter even said there was a time when the angels longed to see what we see clearly. The message of Jesus contained in the Scriptures is a sort of knowledge that should be treasured above everything else we know. Jesus' sacrificial existence is the greatest demonstration of love there has ever been. Learn what his sacrifice means and how it should change your life.

<u>Chapter 3</u>

Love

"So now faith, hope, and love abide, these three; but the greatest of these is love." —1 Corinthians 13:13

If you could transport back in time to the United States in the middle of the nineteenth century, you would find a place isolated by an inability to travel great distances efficiently. There was a strong need for effective transportation that could link major cities thousands of miles apart from one another. A project was born to bring together millions of people, through the Transcontinental Railroad.

"Before the railroad, it took almost six months and cost $1000 to travel between California and New York. After the Transcontinental Railroad was completed, it cost $150 and took one week. For the first time, U.S. Americans could freely travel from coast to coast."[1]

The dangers of more remote areas of the United States limited travel, but with the creation of a Transcontinental Railroad it was much safer and cheaper. After the completion of the railroad, trade became more efficient and more profitable. The United States' economy exploded, becoming a world power by the turn of the twentieth century. The steam engine locomotive was at the heart of this venture. A furnace and boiler work alongside one another to produce the steam necessary for the engine to function. There would be workers, known as fireman, on the train who used shovels to load the fuel into the furnace. Coal, wood, or some other fuel would be force fed into the furnace to keep the locomotive running. Each fuel had its own benefits and properties. Some would burn hotter, longer, or both.

Like trains, there are fuels that drive our actions. We are motivated by a multitude of different desires that cause us to do everything. Some decisions, or actions, are motivated by an anxious fear, selfishness, a desire to be liked, or love. By no means are these the only motivators, but they sum up a number of them.

Insufficient Fuels

Obviously, there are motivators that are better than others. An anxious fear is not a good motivator. Many times we make the wrong decision when we worry about the unlikely possibilities, instead of working to solve the issue. The fear of failure, fear of trying something new, or the fear of not being good enough are insufficient. In fact, they keep you from realizing your potential. God has given us every reason to be confident and bold in His promises. Multiple times Jesus urged his disciples to worry less or not to be afraid altogether. I will concede that we should fear God, but that is because He is beyond anything on this earth. He is Holy. There is no comparison between God and any figment of our imagination. He is worthy of our fear. However, He has empowered us to be His representatives on this earth. God has called His people to abandon fear as a motivator for large life decisions.

It is tempting to do whatever best serves your selfish pursuits in life. Selfishness can bring about strong, decisive action. The problem with selfishness is the loneliness that inevitably follows. No one likes someone who is only concerned about themselves. Selfishness has to be the leading cause for divorce and infidelity. A self-centered individual will end up repelling anyone that gets close enough to see their true colors. That is no way to live. Selfishness, as a motivation, causes a great deal of heartache and should be abandoned as soon as humanly possible.

Love

The fuel, or motivation, that should stand above the rest is love. Countless selfless actions are done each day in the name of love. A man will do some pretty crazy things to impress a girl. A woman will work tirelessly to please the man she loves. A father will spend all of his weekends to make sure his son gets to play the sport he enjoys. I'm sure you could look back and remember something your parent or guardian did for you that showed their love. My mother would always be willing to give up what was hers for my sister and me. I never questioned her love for us, because of the sacrifices she made for our family. When love is the motivating factor, there are no limits to what could be done.

John, in 1 John, made it very clear; we should love because God first loved us. Sure, that sounds nice and seems like good advice; but, is there any merit to John's instruction for Christians? What has God done to deserve our love? Who is God to expect something from me? God deserves our love because of the immense love He has shown us. His love is not confined to words or ideas. Instead, the love of God is like a raging river that keeps flowing endlessly. Brennan Manning wrote in *The Ragamuffin*

Gospel, "I could more easily contain Niagara Falls in a teacup than I can comprehend the wild, uncontainable love of God."[2] Even the most intelligent among us cannot fully comprehend the amazing love of God. His love is never ending and it doesn't fail. God has shown His love for us in some very specific ways which we can know; but, keep in mind the fact that His love is stronger than what we can comprehend. When we come to see the various things God has done for us, we will better be able to love Him and others.

Made In His Image

The most obvious sign of God's love for you is that He made you in His image. This world has a way of deceiving us into believing that we have little value. A large number of people look for ways to disparage others so that they themselves feel better. Slander, gossip, and simple discouragement abound in our society. James (the brother of Jesus) had strong words against speaking negatively toward another human being, because that individual has intrinsic value given to them by their Creator (James 3:9). If we are all made in God's image, we should respect one another and value each other. After all, God does.

Beyond being made in the likeness of God, He made you with specific abilities that set you apart. God designed you with special purposes in mind. He gave you the ability to draw, sing, laugh, or help others. Of course, there are countless other skills God has blessed mankind with. You have blessings from God that make you unique. Don't ever forget that God created you with value. We know David knew this because he wrote in Psalm 139:14, *"I praise you, for I am fearfully and wonderfully made."* In spite of his mistakes, David knew that God making him was an act of love from the Almighty. You are fearfully and wonderfully made. The New

Living Translation is perhaps easier to make sense of, *"Thank you for making me so wonderfully complex!"* You have beauty given to you, by God.

About ten years ago, a family I know was expecting their first child. The joy they felt turned to uncertainty when their doctors presented them with a choice. They were escorted to a grey room with no windows, where doctors told them that their child had Arthrogryposis Multiplex Congenita (AMC). This condition prevents joints from moving, and requires numerous surgeries to give mobility. Without operations and intense care, she would never have been able to anything on her own. The Springs (their family name) were advised to abort their unborn child because of the condition that she would be born with. Arthrogryposis would be something their child would deal with their whole life. They decided against abortion, because of their values. Sadie Spring was born and has had 9 surgeries, casting on her arms and legs, and countless hours of occupational and physical therapy.

In spite of the challenge of arthrogryposis, Sadie lives an adventure-filled life. She runs and plays with all of the other kids. She loves to play outside. She inspires me every time I see her. I honestly don't know of a happier kid! Sadie is now able to show everyone she knows that God blesses each of us with His love. Despite her condition, she is able to experience the goodness of God and show the love of Christ to the world. She even encourages me with the artwork that hangs in my office. Like Sadie, you have been made in a special way. You have gifts that allow you to show God's love to the world. You are fearfully and wonderfully made.

Not only did God make you in a special way, He made you with the purpose of seeking Him. Paul preached boldly to a large crowd at the Areopagus in Athens, Greece.

Acts 17:24-27
The God who made the world and everything in it, being Lord of heaven
and earth, does not live in temples made by man, nor is he served by
human hands, as though he needed anything, since he himself gives to all
mankind life and breath and everything. And he made from one man every
nation of mankind to live on all the face of the earth, having determined
allotted periods and the boundaries of their dwelling place, that they
should seek God, and perhaps feel their way toward him and find him. Yet
he is actually not far from each one of us

God made each of us with a time and place in mind. He put
you where you are for a reason—to seek God. God has given you
the best possible scenario for you to seek Him. How great is the
love of God! He even positioned Himself where He could be found
by mankind. Other religions have gods that are unavailable or too
distant for people to reach them. God has placed Himself within
our reach. We can find Him. Christians have access, through Jesus
and the Holy Spirit, that even the prophets of the Old Testament
could not dream of having. God showed His love for us in how He
made us.

Blessings

Another way God showed His love for us was and is all the
good things He has given to each of us. I'm not really talking about
generic blessings either. Each person has gifts, abilities, and
opportunities that are special to them. I have friends that are good
singers. To encourage others, they travel to other local churches and
worship with them. There are many people that are blessed with
resources, which they use to help those who have less. Some people
that I love dearly don't have any talents that jump out to you, but

they are always there when you need them. They bless other people with their consistency. It is a blessing to know that there are other Christians that are always willing to be there for you. God has shown His love to you through the gifts He has given you.

Additionally, you have people in your life that are a gift from God. My wife, MacKenzie, is a blessing directly from God. She inspires me to serve Him more faithfully, but she also makes me happy. We enjoy spending time together like most married couples do. I love worshipping with her because her voice, which is another gift from God, meshes well with mine to create harmony. There are things about your spouse that make them special to you. Praise God for these sorts of blessings! If you have a house and food for your table, don't take it for granted. Thank God for all these good gifts. James credits "every good and perfect gift" to God (James 1:17). God is the ultimate giver of good things. Every good thing in your life comes from the Almighty, in one way or another.

Gratitude

God wants His people to be joyous and hopeful for the future. While we shouldn't teach a gospel that places preeminence on happiness, God is concerned with our happiness. The life of a Christian is difficult and has its challenges, but in spite of challenges, we can find joy in Christ. We can manufacture our own happiness by God's grace. When I consider what God is doing in my life, I become happy. I take joy in what God is doing in my life. Our unhappiness comes when we fail to be thankful for what we do have. G. K. Chesterton explained what I am floundering about, *"When it comes to life the critical thing is whether you take things for granted or take them with gratitude."* Two people can look at the same set of facts and walk away with two different conclusions.

Gratefulness sees God's love in His gifts to us. The ungrateful heart dwells on what he doesn't have and how hard his current circumstances are. When we don't see God's love displayed in our lives, through what He has given us, we will not serve Him faithfully.

Thankfulness can be seen among those with everything, and those with nothing. Gratitude is a perspective on life that changes how we view the world. You can travel the globe and find thankfulness at every corner. God has shown His love to mankind in ways that should open our eyes. If we want to be the people God wants us to be, we have to be thankful. Consider the following passage:

Colossians 3:14-17
And above all these put on love, which binds everything together in perfect harmony. And let the peace of Christ rule in your hearts, to which indeed you were called in one body. And be thankful. Let the word of Christ dwell in you richly, teaching and admonishing one another in all wisdom, singing psalms and hymns and spiritual songs, with thankfulness in your hearts to God. And whatever you do, in word or deed, do everything in the name of the Lord Jesus, giving thanks to God the Father through him.

Paul wanted the Colossians to be thankful, which we know from the repetition of the concept. The peace in our hearts is a good gift from God, so be thankful. When we are joyful and sing songs, be thankful. Any time we remember what God is doing in our lives, it is appropriate to give thanks. Actually, everything we do in this life should be tied back to Jesus Christ. We really cannot take credit for any of this. The things we do are only possible because of the love of God.

49

The Greatest Gift

God is a giver of good things; He shows His love through these good things He has given us. If we fail to realize what God has done, is doing, and will do, how can we expect to be affected by Him? God has made us in His image, given us good things and last, but most significant, He gave us His Son.

Romans 5:6-8
For while we were still weak, at the right time Christ died for the ungodly. For one will scarcely die for a righteous person—though perhaps for a good person one would dare even to die— but God shows his love for us in that while we were still sinners, Christ died for us.

The greatest display of love is found in the form of Jesus, the Christ. God's willingness to send Jesus to die for His enemies declares, for all time, that He loves mankind. We may be willing to make large sacrifices for those we care about, but I'm not sure any of us would die for those opposed to us. The depth of God's love is here in the text—we were still sinners when Jesus died for us.

Consider this, Jesus lived for about 33 years on this earth. He rubbed shoulders with people from all walks of life. He was born into a carpenter's family, he associated with tax collectors and sinners, and he stood before governing authorities. Jesus was insulted, falsely accused, and generally mistreated. John wrote that Jesus *'knew all people,'* plus he *'knew what was in a man'* (John 2:24-25). There was no deceiving Jesus into thinking that he was dying for a world that was worthy of his love. Yet, he still gave his life. He could have wielded all the powers of Heaven and commanded the angelic armies. He didn't. Jesus submitted to the will of the Father, giving his life as the ransom price for mankind.

The Cross is where we find the best example of love we could ever find.

The fact that mankind did not deserve Jesus' sacrifice shows us another facet of God's love for us. However, it is not the only one to be considered. Read what Paul said later in Romans:

Romans 8:31-34
What then shall we say to these things? If God is for us, who can be against us? He who did not spare his own Son but gave him up for us all, how will he not also with him graciously give us all things? Who shall bring any charge against God's elect? It is God who justifies. Who is to condemn? Christ Jesus is the one who died—more than that, who was raised—who is at the right hand of God, who indeed is interceding for us.

God spared no expense in acquiring His chosen people. Of all the things that God could have done for us, He decided to hold nothing back. He gave His only Son for the world. Do you now see why we have no reason to fear? God is the one who justifies. Jesus is the one appointed to condemn, but he is the one interceding on our behalf. Additionally, the Spirit helps negate our weakness of not knowing how to pray. All the powers of Heaven desire that you be saved through a relationship with God. God's love is shown in how much He was willing to do to save you.

Think about the importance of how we spend our time and money. Godfrey Davies, who wrote a biography about the Duke of Wellington, said, *"I found an old account ledger that showed how the Duke spent his money. It was a far better clue to what he thought was really important than the reading of his letters or speeches."*[3] If I examined your budget and schedule, I could get a pretty good picture of what you value. Transportation, shelter, and food are important needs that can require a great deal of money, but we pay for them because they are essential to our survival. Beyond needs, how much you pay for cable or how little you give to others says something about you. What does God's payment say about His love for you?

1 Peter 1:17-19
And if you call on him as Father who judges impartially according to each one's deeds, conduct yourselves with fear throughout the time of your exile, knowing that you were ransomed from the futile ways inherited from your forefathers, not with perishable things such as silver or gold, but with the precious blood of Christ, like that of a lamb without blemish or spot.

Our salvation came at a high cost. It was not that God had to open the vaults of Heaven to put forward a large sum of money. It wasn't any object that God had to give. God sent, from His Throne Room, the One at His Right Hand. He had to send the Son of His Own Likeness. Silver and gold gain and lose value over time, but the blood of Christ will never depreciate. His blood is beyond physical value. God's love for you is beyond anything we can fully comprehend.

Adoption

The act of sending Jesus to die for the sins of the world has benefits beyond salvation. God's love has brought Christians into His family.

1 John 3:1a
See what kind of love the Father has given to us, that we should be called children of God; and so we are.

Due to our sin, we deserved to die. The Bible is clear on it's teaching of sin. It was God's love and grace that opened the door for us to be with Him, which we have been discussing. The additional grace is found in our place in God's household. John wanted his readers to see the love of God manifested in their sonship. God loved us enough to send Jesus, so that we can be His heirs. We have the privilege of being able to call God our Father. We have the privilege of being able to ask Him for anything we need. We have the privilege of being a part of the family of God, called the Church. We are His Family. *"See what kind of love the Father has given to us!"*

Timothy Keller, in his book *The Prodigal God*, proposed that we have mislabeled the *Parable of the Prodigal Son*. Keller emphasized the lavish (prodigal) love of the father in the parable when he welcomed home the son, who wasted his money in riotous living. Keller made this statement about the importance of what God did for us, through Christ,

"What makes you faithful or generous is not just a redoubled effort to follow moral rules. Rather, all change comes from deepening your understanding of the salvation of Christ and living out of the changes that understanding creates in your heart."[4]

In other words, the more we see and understand the love of God, the more we will be faithful to God. Love is the linchpin that keeps us fastened to God. In John's words, again, *"We love because He first loved us"* (1 John 4:19). God loves us so much. The depth of His love is evident in His willingness to give His Son. Like the Father's love in *The Parable of the Prodigal Son*, the love of God should then cause us to have a deep love for Him. God has welcomed us home.

Our Response

A. W. Tozer wrote about the sacrifice Jesus made on our behalf in *The Crucified Life*,

"Too often, we give God only the tired remnants of our time. If Jesus Christ had given us only the remnant of His time, we would all be on our way to that darkness that knows no morning. Christ gave us not the tattered leftovers of His time; He gave us all the time he had. But some of us give Him only the leftovers of our money and of our talents and never give our time fully to the Lord Jesus Christ who gave us all."[5]

Jesus' sacrifice is one that inspires his followers to give their all to him. The sacrifice that is required on our part should control the rest of our life. God asks for surrender to His way. What exactly does God require for those who wish to follow Jesus? Jesus is basically asked that question in Luke 10.

Luke 10:25-28
And behold, a lawyer stood up to put him to the test, saying, "Teacher, what shall I do to inherit eternal life?" He said to him, "What is written in the Law? How do you read it?" And he answered, "You shall love the Lord your God with all your heart and with all your soul and with all your strength and with all your mind, and your neighbor as yourself." And he said to him, "You have answered correctly; do this, and you will live."

The whole law is boiled down into two commandments. They are echoed in the teachings of Jesus and the apostles, which we will see. Jesus said in Matthew's account of the Gospel that all the Law and the Prophets depend on these commandments. Love God with all that you are; love your neighbor as yourself. God's redemptive plan can be summarized with the same word that can be used to explain our response to Him, love. Neither God's plan of salvation nor our response to God are complicated. In fact, it is quite simple. God's love for us compelled Him to send Jesus. Our love for God should compel us into a committed service of Him. If these commandments are so important, then we should have some concept of their importance.

What Is Love?

Before studying the commands themselves, let us dive into the word love. There are multiple words for love in the New Testament, but the type of love that we are studying is only used for *agape* love. *Agape* is the highest form of love there is, and it is a preferential love. *Agape* love is defined best in 1 Corinthians.

1 Corinthians 13:4-7
Love is patient and kind; love does not envy or boast; it is not arrogant or rude. It does not insist on its own way; it is not irritable or resentful; it does not rejoice at wrongdoing, but rejoices with the truth. Love bears all things, believes all things, hopes all things, endures all things.

Read over that again. If that is truly what love is, why do we use that word so often? We don't mean what this passage says every time we say, "love". Society has hoodwinked us into thinking feelings or emotions are love when they really aren't. Did you notice what kinds of words are used to describe love? Many of the words used are *verbs or describe action*. One of the key aspects of *agape* love is the presence of positive action for another group or individual. You cannot love God, or other people, without action.

Additionally, love is selfless. We see false love in the press and in our entertainment constantly. People split up because "so and so doesn't make me feel special anymore" or "I'm just not feeling it anymore." This false love creeps into our homes as well. We may say, "I love you, but…" then say something incredibly selfish or rude. Do we love someone if we are only looking out for our own interests? Why don't we quit misusing the word love and start pointing out selfishness in our own hearts? When we slow down, and look in the mirror, we can see the problem with how we are acting. To show love we need to be patient, display humility, and be less irritable. Is it hard? Yes. Do not give up. We all need practice thinking less of our selves, and thinking more of others.

Loving God

First of the two great commands, we are commanded to love God with our heart, our soul, our strength, and our mind. This command was first given in the book of Deuteronomy, when Moses was speaking to the people on behalf of God. It was given right after the Ten Commandments were shared with the people. The commandment to love God with everything is right after a list of specific commands. We learn from the close connection between love and commandments that loving God involves listening to Him. Jesus, as well as John, attested to this.

Jesus said in the Gospel of John:
"If you love me, you will keep my commandments" (John 14:15).

"Whoever has my commandments and keeps them, he it is who loves me. And he who loves me will be loved by my Father, and I will love him and manifest myself to him" (John 14:21)

"Jesus answered him, 'If anyone loves me, he will keep my word, and my Father will love him, and we will come to him and make our home with him'" (John 14:23)

"If you keep my commandments, you will abide in my love, just as I have kept my Father's commandments and abide in his love" (John 15:10).

John wrote in his letters:
"And by this we know that we have come to know him, if we keep his commandments" (1 John 2:3).

"For this is the love of God, that we keep his commandments. And his commandments are not burdensome" (1 John 5:3).

"And this is love, that we walk according to his commandments; this is the commandment, just as you have heard from the beginning, so that you should walk in it" (2 John 1:6).

There is an intimate connection between loving God and keeping His commandments. You might even argue that they are the same thing. Ethelbert Stauffer wrote of the submission to God's way in this entry in the Theological Dictionary of the New Testament,

"To love God is to exist for Him as a slave for his lord (cf. Lk. 17:7 ff.). It is to listen faithfully and obediently to His orders, to place oneself under His lordship, to value above all else the realization of this lordship (cf. Mt. 6:33). It also means, however, to base one's whole being on God, to cling to Him with unreserved confidence, to leave with Him all care or final responsibility, to live by His hand. It is to hate and despise all that does

57

not serve God nor come from Him to break with all other ties, to cut away all that hinders (Mt.5:29 f.), to snap all bonds except that which binds to God alone."[6]

Loving God is quite the commitment, but remember how much He was willing to do for you. Consider how great His love is for you.

I know that humanity's inability to keep the rules is the reason that Jesus needed to die. We are no longer measured based upon our own righteousness. Instead, we are covered by the blood of Jesus that washed us clean. Mankind is now able to submit to God, through obedience, to receive the blessings Jesus achieved for us. God desires that our lives be transformed into the image of His Son, Jesus. To love God is to submit to Him completely. Search the Scriptures to see what God would have you do today. Make a commitment to do what the Bible says. Do it God's way.

Loving Our Neighbor

Thankfully, the second great commandment is also explained elsewhere in Scripture. What does it mean to love our neighbor as we love ourselves? The lawyer in Luke 10 asked Jesus who his neighbor was. The parable that Jesus told him cannot be overlooked. This is the point where Jesus told the story of the Good Samaritan. A man was beaten and left for dead along the side of the road. A priest and a Levite walked by without even acknowledging the man's needs. The Samaritan, who would be an adversary to the Jews, helped the man. He put the wounded man on his own animal and paid for him to be helped at an inn. Jesus asked the lawyer who the neighbor was to the man who fell among the robbers. The lawyer was so prejudiced that he wouldn't call him a Samaritan. He simply said, *"The one who showed him mercy"* (Luke 10:37). It is well-known that the Jews would make a wide berth around Samaria to avoid contact with Samaritans. Despite the hatred for the Samaritans among the Jews, Jesus called them neighbors. The love Jesus calls us to show goes beyond racial or religious background. Christians should have a love for humanity like God does. From Jesus' ministry we can see that he worked hard to reach people of all backgrounds. He loved people as he loved himself.

Additionally, in the Sermon on the Mount, Jesus told his disciples, *"Love your enemies and pray for those who persecute you"* (Matthew 5:44). In that context he points out the fact that everyone loves people that love them. It is easy to love someone who loves you. In order to show the sacrificial love of God, we have to love people who don't love us. Remember the love Jesus showed on the cross. He died for the people who put him there. Jesus' act of love was for his enemies.

How do we show love to our neighbor? That would logically be the next question. Since we know our neighbor is anyone we come in contact with, we should try to figure out how we should treat others. Paul has some things to say about this very commandment.

Romans 13:8-10
Owe no one anything, except to love each other, for the one who loves another has fulfilled the law. For the commandments, "You shall not commit adultery, You shall not murder, You shall not steal, You shall not covet," and any other commandment, are summed up in this word: "You shall love your neighbor as yourself." Love does no wrong to a neighbor; therefore love is the fulfilling of the law.

There you have it. Love is concerned with what is best for our neighbor. Paul, like Jesus, explained that all commandments are explained in this one—love your neighbor as yourself. A. T. Robertson said concerning this passage, *"Love is the only solution for our social relations and national problems."*[7] If I love my neighbor, I will not want to kill him. If I love my neighbor, I would want him to enjoy the things that he has worked for; I wouldn't want to take them from him. If I love my neighbor, I wouldn't want to hurt him by taking his wife. Love gives meaning and purpose to all the commandments. The commandments teach us how to love our neighbor. From the commandments, we know how to live peacefully with those around us. God has taught us how to love Him, and how to love our neighbor.

The apostle John raised the stakes on the commandment to love our neighbor by explaining that our proximity to God is based upon how we treat others. In 1 John there are multiple passages that explain that we can say that we are in the light, but if we hate our brother, we are actually in darkness. Earlier in the same letter John explained that God is light and there is no darkness in Him. Yet again, we find a passage from the New Testament that teaches us that our actions are just as important as our words. We can't deceive God. He will know how we think about other people and how we act toward them. God understands our hearts. Wherever you are reading this book, please give thought to how you treat your fellow man. Your treatment of others can keep you from spending eternity with God.

The two great commandments—love God and love our neighbor as ourselves—encapsulate every kind of command God has given us. The relationship between the two is significant. The two commands are not in an either/or situation. Either you love God or you love your neighbor. Instead, you must both love God and your neighbor. God expects His people to do right by others. After all, each of us is made in His image. Your enemies and those who hurt you are still made with intrinsic value. When God values someone, we should too. The things, or people, that are important to Him should be important to us.

There is one final point I want to consider in connection with love. *"Anyone who does not love does not know God, because God is love"* (1 John 4:8). *God is love.* Mankind's entire purpose in life is to glorify the God who made us. Our decision—to love or not to love—determines whether or not we live up to that purpose. How can someone glorify a God, who defines Himself with love, by showing hatred? In reality, it is impossible. On the flip side, what greater way is there to glorify God than to love? There isn't. When we truly love others, by doing right by them, God is on display in us. We show Christ to the world through our love. As Christians, we should find no greater joy than helping someone else to see who Jesus is. Love is at the core of who God is. We can see that in all He has done for us, as well as every person on the earth.

Almost exactly 150 years ago, the Transcontinental Railroad was completed. Steam powered engines revolutionized American travel. In a much larger way, if the Church of Jesus Christ was motivated by a burning, intense love for God and mankind, the world would be changed. We would fulfill the words of Jesus, by showing others that we are His, by our love. We wouldn't be able to welcome people fast enough because countless multitudes would want to be a part of a selfless, loving group of God's people. Perhaps it is a lack of love that keeps our numbers small. A Church, with the two great commands as their battle cry, would easily overcome the Evil One. The Devil could carry no weapon that would be able to stand against us. God—being love—carries us through the battle, giving us ultimate victory.

Chapter 4

Faith

"I don't know what the future may hold, but I know who holds the future." —Ralph Abernathy

The game is on the line. The score is tied. Who is taking the last shot? No matter who takes it, the whole team is depending on one person to win the game.

The business has been on a losing streak. They have been outbid for the last few projects; they're running out of options. There is one last presentation to gain new work. A group is chosen to work on it. The best orator is chosen to make the presentation. Everyone in the company is counting on them to make the difference.

I was in Boy Scouts for much of my younger life. Whenever we competed at Camporees we had different scouts that were good at different things. As you might expect, we had some guys who loved to play with fire. We had some who liked telling stories. We had some that were good at knot tying. Each person was counted on for doing well in their event.

Whether you think about it or not, you have been practicing having faith your whole life. In each of the above scenarios a group is putting their faith in an individual, or a small group of their peers. With all of this practice of putting our faith in others, a disturbing question comes to mind. *Why do we have a hard time having faith in God?* We trust people because of their skills that they have worked on and their natural abilities. What makes God worthy of our trust? What sort of abilities does He have?

The first question—*What makes Him worthy of our trust?*—is really not the right question to be asking. It is egocentric. God is not centered on us. Instead, we should be centered on Him. God existed before we did. He made us in His Image, not the other way around. He demands our trust and reverential fear, because He made us. The beautiful fact is that God wants to welcome us into His family.

Secondly, God is the self-described Almighty One. Instead of what God can do, it would be easier to compile a list of what God cannot do. Obviously, God cannot lie or sin; but, when it comes to the ability to help His people, there is no limit to His competency. God is able to help. In this chapter we will examine some of the ways God helped in the past.

It is possible that we have gotten ahead of ourselves. We should go back a little bit to ask the question—What is faith? Thankfully, the Bible defines what faith is in Hebrews 11:1, *"Now faith is the assurance of things hoped for, the conviction of things not seen."* This definition of faith teaches us that it is far from a blind shot in the dark.

While it is true that we cannot see God, Paul made it clear that God's invisible attributes are seen in the created universe (Romans 1). In other words we can see what God has done, thereby having proof of His existence. The created world around us is full of proofs for the existence of an Intelligent Maker. There is an order in the cosmos which is impossible to produce, given natural circumstances. The human body surprises scientists with its complexity to this very day. How can a body as complex as the human body develop through natural means? Not only the body, but the very dimensions of the cosmos. Earth is just the right distance from the sun to permit life, and it revolves at the correct speed to allow for the seasons needed for plant growth. The force of gravity is a precise number that organisms can tolerate. J. P. Moreland wrote about the astounding improbabilities in his book *Love Your God With All Your Mind*.

> "In a phrase: the universe is precisely fine-tuned so life could appear. Over thirty independent, hard facts about the universe have been discovered in the form of basic constants of nature that are, scientifically speaking, brute facts and for which there is no further scientific explanation (the force of gravity in the universe, the charge of an electron, the rest mass of a proton, the rate of expansion resulting from the big bang). What blows the minds of so many is that if any single one of these —much less all thirty!—had been slightly larger or smaller on the order of a billionth of a percentage point, then no life could have appeared in the universe. The universe is a razor's edge of precisely balanced life-permitting conditions."[1]

It is not just unlikely that life formed from nothing, it is statistically impossible. Creation itself witnesses to the wisdom of its Creator.

We can also have an assurance in the existence of God by studying His word. The Bible is a magnificent volume written by a few dozen men over the span of centuries, separated by great distances. Their archaeological accuracy is unparalleled in antiquity. There are literally thousands of manuscripts and papyri that testify to one another, to verify the validity of what was written. The providence it took to preserve the Bible contributed to its divine origin.

While we may have a lot of facts that can cause someone to conclude that there is a God, we don't see actually see God. There is still a need for a trust, or faith, in God. We can be thankful that God wants to help with that. We are going to see that He wants you to believe in Him. He is trying to grab hold of your attention.

Building Faith

When people talk about faith, they assume it takes complete effort from the one having faith. They think that they have to muster up enough faith in order to please God. Or they might think their faith is lacking. I know some people that struggle with this. One thing you might not have considered is that God is looking to build faith in His people. He is not making the decision for us, but He is helping us along.

If we go back to the book of Exodus, we will see an instance where God helps His people's faith grow. The Israelites had just left slavery in Egypt. God had promised that He would bless them with a land that was prosperous in every way. There were still some challenges the Israelites had to face, before they reached the Promised Land.

Exodus 13:17-18
"When Pharaoh let the people go, God did not lead them by way of the land of the Philistines, although that was near. For God said, "Lest the people change their minds when they see war and return to Egypt." But God led the people around by the way of the wilderness toward the Red Sea. And the people of Israel went up out of the land of Egypt equipped for battle."

65

This passage may not seem like much on the surface, but there are some key details that give away God's intentions. The more obvious detail is God was protecting His people from war. He knew that they would be disturbed and scared. They were not ready to see battle, because it would cause them to go back to Egypt. God knew what they needed. That leads to the second observation, which is more subtle. He led them to the banks of the Red Sea. The people encamped where there was no place to hide. Soon after, the Egyptian army hurried toward the people of Israel. They were against the Sea, and the army came toward them. Being a nation of at least a million people, there was no way for them to move quickly. Many of the Israelites would have been older people or young children, who could not travel very fast. At that moment, all hope was lost until God showed His hand. He divided the waters before the opposing army could attack. The Israelites walked through the Sea on dry ground; the rest is history.

Consider for a second though, *God led them to the Red Sea*. Let that sink in. When the Israelites were at the edge of the Sea, they were terrified because they could see the army was coming at them. They cried out for help, and didn't know what to do. This was the moment that Moses declared the salvation of the Lord. It was time for Moses's faith to shine in the face of adversity. For the others, it was an opportunity for God to build faith in them. From the splitting of the Red Sea, many of the Israelites grew to have faith in God. Of course, their faithfulness would be tested; but, God was doing his part to ensure they had an opportunity to see His Mighty Hand.

Exodus 14:30-31
Thus the Lord saved Israel that day from the hand of the Egyptians, and
Israel saw the Egyptians dead on the seashore. Israel saw the great power
that the Lord used against the Egyptians, so the people feared the Lord,
and they believed in the Lord and in his servant Moses.

Power brought about faith. When the Israelites witnessed God's power, they believed. When we realize the power of God, all else makes sense. I need to come to the realization that I need to learn from the Supreme Being of the universe. Through His love, He has taught me to love. So, I will love. He has taught me from past experiences to trust Him. God did the same for Moses. Do you remember where Moses started out? He had excuse after excuse when God originally called Him. After he saw God's power through the plagues and the signs He gave him, he came to faith. Though we need faith to be pleasing to God, we need to stand in awe of who He is before we come to a strong faith in Him. Your faith in your favorite player or co-worker is dependent upon how capable they are. Likewise, our faith in God is dependent upon how strong we think He is. When we have a high view of God's transformative power, we will have great faith in what He can do. God has done great things, which are seen in His Creation. He has also made a difference in countless lives. He has blessed you immensely. Be thankful for what He has done.

Take comfort in the fact that God is working to build faith in you. Everything that He has done contributes to the case for your belief in Him. Difficulty in this life is inevitable. There is not a person on this Earth that can escape the troubles of life, due to sin. However, the one who has faith can trust in God's eternal plan. I know that God can use the difficulties in our lives for good. There are too many instances in the Scriptures where the prophets and preachers declared the importance of hardship. Challenges bring about the skill of perseverance and this perseverance gives us hope for the future. God is faithful.

1 Corinthians 10:12-13
"Therefore let anyone who thinks that he stands take heed lest he fall. No temptation has overtaken you that is not common to man. God is faithful, and he will not let you be tempted beyond your ability, but with the temptation he will also provide the way of escape, that you may be able to endure it."

There is not a promise in this passage that will shield us from challenges. Instead, God offers a way of escape to endure the difficulty. I love this passage because it is written to all Christians. If you are mature, take heed lest you fall. If you are struggling and perhaps immature, rely on the promise that God will provide a way to endure. All of this hinges on the statement, "God is faithful." Not only is God the Almighty, He is faithful to His people.

When you are going through a hard time, you don't have to question whether or not God will see you through it. The real question is, What is God doing in this situation? Hardship, whether it be financial, health-related, or loss, has a way of showing us our own weakness. George Müller is credited for saying, *"Faith does not operate in the realm of the possible. There is no glory for God in that which is humanly possible. Faith begins where man's power ends."* Those times of need can be the point when you see clearly how much God is doing in your life. The times I have felt closest to God were when I was doing things I never thought I could do. God enables us to go outside of our comfort zone to accomplish His will.

Müller, who was quoted above, is an excellent example of having a strong faith in what God can do. He founded orphanages in England. In 1836, he started out by housing 30 girls in his own home. In just over 30 years, that number grew to a staggering 2,000 children between 5 separate orphanages. While that is impressive, one fact takes it to another level.

"Through all this, Müller never made requests for financial support, nor did he go into debt, even though the five homes cost a total of over £100,000 to build. Many times, he received unsolicited food donations only hours before they were needed to feed the children, further strengthening his faith in God."[2]

When Müller spoke about God being glorified in the impossible, he had experienced it firsthand. God, through providence, strengthened Muller's faith.

Doubt

The Lord even wants to help those who may initially have doubts. When you examine the Gospel message, you realize how important the resurrection is. God showed all of mankind that He had the power over death, by raising Jesus. From the resurrection, we learn of the hope of eternal life that Christians have to look forward to. Our resurrection from death to life will be like Jesus' resurrection. Paul will go so far as to say that if the resurrection didn't happen, Christians should be the object of pity. People should feel sorry for us without the resurrection. We know from the testimonies of Christians that Jesus was actually raised. Paul's strong words underscore the importance of Jesus being raised from the dead. Did you know that there were those who doubted the resurrection? You probably did know that because one of the twelve has been labeled "Doubting Thomas."

We do not really know much about Thomas. He is one of the original twelve apostles called by Jesus and he is present consistently when the disciples are named. On one occasion, Thomas was somewhere else. It just so happened to be the day that Jesus rose again. I don't really know what it is, but exciting things always seem to happen when I leave a room. I may be watching sports or a movie, inevitably, I miss something important. I feel sympathy for Thomas. The one time he was gone something amazing happened. The disciples were gathered together in a locked room. The Bible made it clear that they were afraid of the Jews. Suddenly, Jesus appeared in the room with the apostles. They were glad to see the Lord, who blessed them and gave them the Holy Spirit.

Imagine the emotional roller coaster the apostles were experiencing, of which Thomas was one. The week before, crowds welcomed Jesus into Jerusalem with palm branches. It seemed like everyone loved Jesus. In a span of a few days, he is arrested, tried, and killed on a cross. He was in the tomb for a few days, and those days had to be challenging for the apostles. They were alone and on the run from the Jewish authorities, who wanted to defeat Christ's plans. The apostles had gone from the highest high of riding Jesus' coattails to the low depression of apparent defeat. To Thomas, wouldn't it seem sick to joke about seeing the Lord? I have to think he felt anger and frustration over the situation.

A week after Jesus' resurrection, the disciples gathered together again. This time Thomas was with them. Jesus appeared to them with the same message of peace as before. This time he directs his attention to Thomas, who had missed the previous meeting. Thomas had made a rash commitment to never believe unless he saw the place where the nails were driven and touched the side of Jesus. Jesus, being God, knew of his vow. He instructed him to put his hands in his side and encouraged him not to disbelieve, but to believe. I find it powerful what Jesus did not say in this instance. He could have been harsh with Thomas, calling him a faithless servant. He could have told him not to let the door hit him on the way out. Instead, Jesus patiently helped him to overcome his unbelief. This is another example of God desiring to build faith in His people. His doubts did not disqualify him from a place in Jesus' kingdom. Instead, Jesus helped Thomas to overcome his doubts. Thomas exclaimed, *"My Lord and my God!"* He knew that this man was the risen Lord, after he had seen and touched Jesus.

There are times that we have doubts like Thomas. We may say things like, "I'll believe it when I see it." Often, these kinds of vows are made when other people let us down. We may lack faith when we think the odds are stacked against us. I think we have all faced situations where we would get discouraged and didn't think there was a good way forward. The instances when we feel discouragement are the times that we should have the most faith in what God can do. Abraham and Sarah were too old to have a child, yet they did. Daniel was the perfect meal for the lions, yet God shut their mouths. Shadrach, Meshach, and Abednego weren't wearing fire retardant suits, yet they did not burn in the fire. Time and time again, God aimed to build faith in His people when it seemed like there was no way to escape the difficulty. I know that God can use the hard situation you are in to help you grow in your faith.

Faith Or Fear

What do you fear? What genuinely makes you afraid? There are plenty of things we can be afraid of. The possibilities are truly limitless. As we have already seen, fear is not a good thing to have controlling you. It can keep you from reaching the potential God has waiting for you. I'm going to argue that, generally speaking, there are two ways of approaching a situation. We can have fear or faith. Every one of us has encountered a troubling situation where we did not know the outcome. Those problems are the ones we need to take to God. Pray about them, and let Him handle them.

The Church I work with has always been struggling with the size of our facility. We can never seem to have a building that we fit in. The congregation began meeting in homes for a time. From there, they moved to a hotel conference room. That is where I began partnering with them. It was special to worship in a small room packed to the walls. The next logical step was some small commercial space to rent, which we did. The new place was 1,000 square feet, where we could have a meeting room for maybe 60 people. The Lord blessed us with a landowner, who was a man of faith; and, he also happened to own other properties. Another of his properties was vacated, so we toured the facility. It took some retrofitting, but we were able to make this new facility work and it was just shy of 2,000 square feet. This is where the real issue of space became apparent. We did all we could to make the assembly room as big as possible. We had one friends and family day with 90 people there. So many new people were coming to hear the Gospel and study His word. It was a blessed time of growth. God was causing all of our efforts to grow; we were confident that God had bigger plans for our work.

There were a lot of us constantly looking for new properties. Our kids didn't have adequate classroom space and there were classes that we needed to offer, but we couldn't. There was a time, of at least six months, that I was very discouraged. I didn't think we would ever make the next step. Shamefully, there were times I lacked faith in what God could do. I tell you this because of what happened next. In the middle of this process, I had started looking at Craigslist for facilities in addition to the other sites. It was there that I found a former church building that was three times the size of the building we had at the time. It just so happened that it was less than a mile down the road. The owner was willing to negotiate a price we could pay, and the congregation moved in a few short months later. Through providence, we found a listing off the beaten path so there wasn't a long line of other people who would have been able to beat us to it. God answered our prayers. Our situation changed in a ridiculously short amount of time. We had 123 the first Sunday in the new building. God was faithful. Since then, we have had many services with more than 150 souls. God is continuing to bless our efforts. I have confidence now that God was preparing us for the right time to move so that we would be ready to handle the new needs we would have.

I should have had more faith in what God could do. From that experience, I know to trust in what God has planned. If I'm working toward something God wants me to pursue, He will make it happen. The same is true for you. Have faith in what the Lord will do in your life. There are so many Christians who can tell story after story of God delivering them from hardship. God is faithful.

There is something to learn from the mistakes of others. It's important not to fall into the same traps. We should pick up with the children of Israel, because they still have more to teach us. After the Lord delivered them from the Egyptians, they were making their way toward the Promised Land. It came time for them to send spies into the land to explore it. Twelve spies were sent in and they reported back what they saw. They spoke of how great the land was. The spies brought back some of its fruit. One cluster of grapes had to be carried on a pole by two men. Not only was the fruit large, the land's inhabitants were frightening. At least that's what the spies said.

There were two spies who had a different perspective though. Caleb—one of the faithful spies—encouraged the people, *"But Caleb quieted the people before Moses and said, 'Let us go up at once and occupy it, for we are well able to overcome it'" (Numbers 13:30).* Caleb had complete faith in what God could do with their army. He was not afraid of what might happen. He knew the mighty power of God. After all, he had seen the plagues in Egypt that the Lord used to deliver them. He had seen the Lord split the Red Sea. He had eaten some of the manna and quail in the wilderness that the Lord provided. He had drunk the water the Lord gave them from a rock. There was no question in Caleb's mind about whether or not God could give them this land. He was ready to go; sadly, not everyone felt that way.

Numbers 13:31-32
"Then the men who had gone up with him said, 'We are not able to go up against the people, for they are stronger than we are.' So they brought to the people of Israel a bad report of the land that they had spied out, saying, 'The land, through which we have gone to spy it out, is a land that devours its inhabitants, and all the people that we saw in it are of great height.'"

It was at this point that fear gripped the people. They began to complain and mourn, because they thought they were going to die in the wilderness. They decided to go back to Egypt with a new leader. They made a decision out of fear. Moses, Aaron, Joshua, and Caleb tried to convince the people that God could give them the land, which He had promised. They had great faith in what the Lord could do and they knew that He would keep His promises. These men instructed them not to be afraid but the people wouldn't listen. All of the people were ready to stone the leaders with stones. There are so many things this passage teaches us.

First of all, fear leads us away from faith. Consider this, all twelve spies were dealing with the same set of facts. They all saw how big the people were and how large their armies were. Additionally, they all had experienced God's recent deliverance from the Egyptians, from hunger, and from thirst. Fear clouded the decision making of ten of the twelve spies. They were focusing on their own limitations, rather than what God could do through them. Joshua and Caleb were concerned with the fact that God was on their side, and He had promised to give them the land. In their minds, once God said it, it was going to happen if they had faith. Joshua and Caleb saw the potential for blessing, while the others saw the potential for destruction.

Don't let your fears get in the way of the faith God wants you to have. Another lesson from the story from Numbers is fear leads away from the will of God. God does not want you to be constantly afraid of what is next. He wants you to find peace and joy in Him. His love can surround us, giving us hope for the future. The apostle John wrote about this very thing. God has love for mankind, which He showed in His willingness to sacrifice Christ.

1 John 4:16-18
So we have come to know and to believe the love that God has for us. God is love, and whoever abides in love abides in God, and God abides in him. By this is love perfected with us, so that we may have confidence for the day of judgment, because as he is so also are we in this world. There is no fear in love, but perfect love casts out fear. For fear has to do with punishment, and whoever fears has not been perfected in love.

1 John 5:4
For everyone who has been born of God overcomes the world. And this is
the victory that has overcome the world—our faith.

I cannot say it any better than John. God's love gives us
victory and confidence for the day of judgement. Our fear is not
founded in love. When we love God, through our service to Him,
we can rest in His love for us. God desires that we have confidence
in Him. It is not about how good or special we are, but how
awesome He is. Caleb knew that God had the power to give them
the land, which introduces the last lesson to consider.

When we live by fear, we aren't going to experience all that
we could. The generation that was afraid died in the wilderness.
They did not get to see the Promised Land. Forty years later, God
used Joshua to lead the people into the land He promised them all
those years beforehand. God was ready and able to give it to the
Israelites, after they initially sent in the spies. The Israelites' lack of
faith caused them to miss out and suffer destruction.

What is your fear keeping you from experiencing? Have
faith in how God can bless your conversations. Have faith in how
God can shape your vision. Have faith in the opportunities that
God can open for you.

One of the major reasons that we let fear hold us back is our
inability to look beyond the present moment. Right now it seems
like that person we are worried about will never listen, or they will
never get better. We forget about the transformative power of God.
He has the ability to take the worst of sinners and make saints out
of them. The moment we stop believing that God can change
people is the moment the devil has power over us. Christians
should remind themselves daily of the great power God can have
in our lives and the lives of other people. There are many examples

in the Bible of people with horrible beginnings. God brought about change in prostitutes, demon-possessed men, Nicodemus, and Saul of Tarsus. When we put on the glasses of faith, we see what people can be rather than what they are. Jesus saw people that way.

In churches, or any group for that matter, there is a temptation to be less friendly to those who do not act like us. The single mother with outrageous children, the homeless man, or the man with the trashy mouth can often be brushed aside. We might even create an atmosphere that doesn't welcome people that are different from us. They might get the cold shoulder. Even worse, we might ask them to leave. How did Jesus treat the one stuck in sin? How did Jesus conduct himself to those with nothing? He showed grace and mercy to them. In no way did he overlook their sin, but he was kind to them. He did right by them, because he knew what they could be. Why do you think he stopped Saul on the road to Damascus? He knew that this opponent of the Church could someday be one of its greatest allies. Half of our New Testament would look completely different without the writings of a murderer. Christians should look to the future and the power of God. He can change people into the image of His son. Thankfully, that is what He did for me. Before Christ, I was lost, broken, and hopeless. We have to have faith and emphasize what God can do, rather than focus on where things stand today.

Promises

In stark contrast to our impulses toward fear, God has provided us with promises that give us immense hope for the future. Fear is a constant obstacle in our lives. We may suppress it, but it is still there. God wants to give us so much hope for the future that it swallows our fears. Jesus encouraged his disciples to let go of their fears and believe in God. I'm going to share some promises from Romans 8 with you. When these promises are internalized, our faith will ascend to another level.

Romans 8:1
There is therefore now no condemnation for those who are in Christ Jesus.

Romans 8:15
For you did not receive the spirit of slavery to fall back into fear, but you have received the Spirit of adoption as sons, by whom we cry, "Abba! Father!"

Romans 8:18
For I consider that the sufferings of this present time are not worth comparing with the glory that is to be revealed to us.

Romans 8:26
Likewise the Spirit helps us in our weakness. For we do not know what to pray for as we ought, but the Spirit himself intercedes for us with groanings too deep for words.

Romans 8:32
He who did not spare his own Son but gave him up for us all, how will he not also with him graciously give us all things?

Romans 8:37
No, in all these things we are more than conquerors through him who loved us.

Each of these promises give Christians new hope for the future. Christians are not condemned anymore. We are given new life. We have received the Spirit of adoption, which means we are now welcomed into the household of God. We are now co-heirs of God's promises, with Christ. Paul points to the fact that the sufferings of this life do not compare with the glory that God has in store for us. God gave the Holy Spirit to intercede for us. We are not able to communicate what we need, and the Spirit interprets it into what we need to say. On top of all of this, Paul takes us back to the cross to remind us of how much God truly loves us. He was willing to go so far as to give up His only begotten Son. In all of the situations of life, we are more than conquerors.

There really is no greater list of promises than the one you will find in the book of Romans. Christians should have every available hope for the future. These promises were the ones that the apostles had faith in, which gave them the strength to die a martyrs death. They knew that God had better things in store for them. If you are in Christ, you have the same promises of a place with God and blessings from God that the early Christians had. No matter what we face, we can have faith in what God will do. Corrie ten Boom once said, *"No pit is so deep that He is not deeper still; with Jesus, even in our darkest moments the best remains, and the very best is yet to be."* She is exactly right. There is nothing in this life that God cannot pull us through. Our hope is for future blessings from God, namely eternal life, that no man can take away from us.

Corrie ten Boom and her family helped Jews escape Nazis by hiding them in their home. She helped coordinate a network of people working to aid those whom the Nazis wanted. The Nazis were informed of what was going on in their home and raided it. Corrie spent time in a concentration camp before being released. When she talks about a pit, she understands human suffering. I can't imagine the horrors that she witnessed and experienced in her lifetime.[3]

If you are in Christ, the best things are still to come. You have every reason for hope for the future. Money problems, health issues, and relationship difficulties are not eternal. Our hope is beyond all of those challenging situations. God has given us greater promises to fixate on. Your life will change when you think about these promises daily. You will begin to worry less about things that don't ultimately matter, and you will have peace. Whenever you are struggling, go back to these promises we have studied. You will again find comfort in them. The best things are still to come!

Growth

When I was in Scouts we would really do some stupid things. For example, we had a kid get stabbed in the leg because we played tackle football with knives in our pockets. There was another time when I walked on thin ice. We were camping in the Winter, and it was pretty cold outside. Where we were camping didn't stay cold though, so the ice on lakes was never very thick. There were a couple of us who wanted to impress our friends. We tested the edges of the ice and began to walk on the lake. After a few steps, we started jumping on the ice. Thankfully, nothing came from that experience, other than a good scolding from the troop leaders. While I don't suggest walking on thin ice, I think it's a good illustration for our growth. We may be hesitant to trust God at first. We may check the ice so to speak. The difference with the ice in my story and God is the fact that God is the most solid foundation there is. God is immovable. He is the only One that cannot fail us. The more we see that He helps us and takes care of us, the more we will trust Him. Even though you may not have a strong faith today, your faith can grow.

Abram is a good example of faith growth. God gave him many promises of prosperity, which Abram believed. God told him to leave his homeland. He did. One of his next great tests was in Egypt where he showed his doubt by lying to Pharaoh about his wife, Sarai. Once Pharaoh is afflicted from the Lord he sends Abram and Sarai away from Egypt. Abram prospered during this time but he continued childless. The most significant of God's promises required that he would have a large number of children. Abram could not have children by Sarai, so she gave him her handmaid. Hagar, Sarai's handmaid, gave Abram a son; but, God confirmed that he was not the son of promise. God changed Abram's name to Abraham when He renewed the promise of a great nation to come through him. Abraham finally had the blessed son of promise when he was one hundred years old. When his son Isaac was a young man, God commanded him to go sacrifice him on an altar. Abraham didn't waste time; instead, he rose early in the morning to go offer Isaac. God prevented Abraham from slaying his son at the final moments, even though he was willing to do it. God tested Abraham and he passed.

I believe God used all of these events to help Abraham's faith to grow. Abraham didn't fully trust God early in his journey. He made decisions that revealed hesitations and impatience. However, he did not give up altogether. He stayed the course. His faith grew with all the time he had on this earth. If God had asked him to do something as bold as sacrifice Isaac in the beginning, I'm not sure he would have done it. God knew that Abraham needed time to grow. When it came time for the most difficult thing he had to do, Abraham was ready to have complete faith in God. The writer of the book of Hebrews claimed that Abraham thought God was going to raise Isaac from the dead. What amazing faith!

Like Abraham, we have all made some mistakes and doubted God's providential care. Abraham does not seem to be the smartest man or the wealthiest, but that is not what God expected from him. God wanted him to be obedient and faithful. Ira North eloquently explains this concept. *"God does not require that we be big, or wealthy, or powerful, or super smart. What our Heavenly Father requires is faithfulness."*[4] Abraham was faithful over the long haul. We too need to remain faithful. North quiets our fears of inadequacy with his encouragement to remain faithful above any need to be good enough. After all, we are saved by grace through faith. Our faith, like our love, drives us into greater service. We should have great faith in what God can do through us! We may not see all of the answers right away, but we know that God does. We don't need to know all of what the future holds, but we need to know God—who does hold the future. He knows the way forward, and we need to trust Him with our lives. He has done great things to deserve our honor and faith.

Chapter 5

Worship

"True worship, worship that is pleasing to God, radiates throughout a person's entire life." A. W. Tozer[1]

It couldn't get any better. People were shouting and praising Jesus as the Anointed One of God. He came in riding a colt, while the people were laying down their coats shouting, *"Hosanna!"* They were waving palm branches in adoration of Jesus. I don't know how anyone could detract from the moment, but the religious leaders found fault in him. They rebuked Jesus and commanded that he stop the people from worshipping him, because he was just a man. Jesus made a statement that resonates to this very day, *"He answered, 'I tell you, if these were silent, the very stones would cry out'"* (Luke 19:40).

We should all be humbled by the fact that the stones would cry out if the people did not. Even creation itself, and the stones on the ground, know who God is. There are few statements in Scripture that are clearer on the authority and majesty of Jesus. Through his miracles we see that the spirits and the elements obey him. Now, at his presence the stones would cry out in worship to him. May we never hear the stones crying in our community! May there always be a place where God is worshipped! He is entirely

worthy of the praise of all of His creation. As humans, we are the
pinnacle of what God made, because He made us in His image.
With the image of God, we receive the responsibility of glorifying
him. Our purpose in life is to bring honor and glory to the One who
made us.

I started this book by talking about the power of God. Before
we can do anything else or understand anything from God, we
must recognize how powerful, how majestic, and how holy He is. It
is at that point we know we must run to Him. We have to fall down
before Him, pleading for His mercy. Thankfully, He has always
desired a relationship with His creation. God has done great things
on our behalf. He sent Jesus to die for our sins so that we might be
reconnected with Him. He has blessed you and me with countless
blessings that draw us closer to Him. The only appropriate
response to His holiness and power is worship.

Worship is the exaltation of something of value to you,
which means you can worship basically anything you perceive. You
can value your emotions, your relationships, or your possessions
above other things. Almost anything could be an object of worship,
even our own selves. In reality, self has the greatest chance of
taking God's rightful place in our lives. If you want to determine
what you worship, calculate what you spend your money on and
what you spend your time doing. Our time and money are the two
great currencies we are given in this life. What we spend those
currencies on will end up being what we value or worship.

I'm going to show my hand before we get too far into this
chapter. If you want to find conviction in the Cross of Christ, you
will understand the importance of worshipping God and the place
it should have in your life. The beautiful thing though is worship is
also the vehicle through which we grow. When we spend time in
His word, we are worshipping. When we are talking about the

Bible and what God has done for us, we are worshipping. When we are sharing the Gospel with someone, who has never heard it before, we are worshipping. When we are praying to the Lord, asking Him for what we need and thanking him for what we have, we are worshipping. Many of these things are known as the spiritual disciplines. These disciplines, at their very core, place God in the highest place. We discipline our body to do one of these things. In so doing, we submit to God's plan and purpose instead of our own.

Priorities

How we use our time affects our relationships or hobbies. You may not spend time with a friend anymore because you have been spending more time with your family. Or, perhaps, you spend less time with family because of your job. It is possible you gave up a hobby because other things took the bulk of your available time. If we reduced this issue to its core, we are valuing some things over other things. When money is scarce, hours at work are critical to providing more for your family. When you are struggling to connect with your spouse, you cannot neglect time together to repair your marriage. Time management is one of the more challenging concepts to master in our lives. I think we can all agree that what we spend our time doing speaks volumes about what we feel to be important. What should you value? What should you spend your time on?

We have already studied the greatest command, which is to love God with all of our being. *Agape* love in the Scriptures is a love of priority. If we are going to love God, He has to take the highest place in our hearts. Timothy Keller explained it this way in his book *The Reason For God*, *"Sin is not simply doing bad things, it is putting good things in the place of God. So the only solution is not simply to change our behavior, but to reorient and center the entire heart and life on God."*[2]

Our entire lives and focus are given over in service to God. We follow the pattern of Christ, who was consumed with 'his Father's business.' Paul explained, as a Christian, you must *"present your bodies as a living sacrifice, holy and acceptable to God, which is your spiritual worship" (Romans 12:1b)*. Your life is no longer your own. Mankind's purpose is to give their lives to God, as a life filled with the worship of the Father. As Tozer wrote in *The Purpose of Man*, *"True worship, worship that is pleasing to God, radiates throughout a person's entire life."*[3] When we submit to the will of God, we are worshipping Him. In essence, we are saying God's will is more important to me than whatever I desire to do. We have placed His will above our own. A large portion of our time should be spent in service to God. If we are going to say what we spend our time on is what we value, God deserves it. Actually, we're going to see He should get all of it.

When we gather as a church, we show our desire to place God in the highest where He belongs. The Church of the first century met on the first day of the week. Meeting on Sunday is symbolic for the priority God should be in our life. He gets the best of what we have. We start our week His way. How can you say you love God and not gather with the Church that God ordained to praise Him? You can't. To love God, you must spend your time meeting with the Church, whose primary focus is to give glory and praise to God.

Loving and worshipping God transcends Church gatherings. In fact, I think one of the biggest reasons why many churches are struggling is because they have focused for far too long on what the corporate worship should look like, and have not spent enough time considering what individual worship should look like. In America specifically, it is socially acceptable to go to Church on Sunday and live an actively sinful life the other days of the week. This compartmentalization occurs when we limit the worship of God to our meeting times. When worshipping and serving God encompasses our life, we can't live selfishly and live for God. They are incompatible. Our life is wrestled into submission when it is seen through the lens of worship to God.

Jesus encountered people who worshipped God in vain. They had limited their relationship with God to the mechanical acts of religious service.

Mark 7:6-7
"And he said to them, "Well did Isaiah prophesy of you hypocrites, as it is written, 'This people honors me with their lips, but their heart is far from me; in vain do they worship me, teaching as doctrines the commandments of men.'"

He characterized their worship as vain. It was empty; it had no meaning. When our hearts are far from God, the acts that we call worship hold no value. We can call it whatever we want but if our heart is not in it, God is not pleased with it. Worship to God involves action and attitude. It is essential that we fix our eyes on the Lord, and order our lives in the way that He would prescribe. As we are going to see, worship involves directing our whole life and purpose toward God. Serving Him will become the primary objective, and all else will begin to seem trivial.

Paul wrote in his first known letter to the Corinthians about some issues they were struggling with. There was division over the subject of eating meat offered to idols. He gave his argument on the topic and concluded with this instruction, *"So, whether you eat or drink, or whatever you do, do all to the glory of God" (1 Corinthians 10:31).* The pertinent definition of the Greek word used for glory is to *"honor as enhancement or recognition of status or performance."*[4] To give glory to God is to recognize His importance as the greatest Being there is. After all, He is the origin of all things that exist in reality.

When Paul wrote that we are to glorify God with everything that we do, he was saying that all of our actions should show that God is worthy of praise. To glorify God is to lift him up. Paul moved quickly beyond eating and drinking to capture every single action, and commanded that it all give honor to God. This concept takes us back to what Tozer wrote about how worship should involve our whole self. We should consistently ask ourselves what would bring honor and glory to God. If what we do does not, shouldn't we discard it? Our time and our energy should be devoted to bringing glory to God. As we move forward, we are going to see how that takes place, what kind of activities we should involve ourselves in, and how far-reaching our worship should be.

Daily Worship

You may be asking yourself, "How can I do everything to the glory of God?" I ask myself that question on a consistent basis. What we aren't taking into account is the comprehensive nature of the Scriptures. We know what the Scriptures teach about money, jobs, relationships, and our daily life. If we are living in accordance with what God preserved in the Bible, are we not worshipping God? When we follow what God's word says, we are telling the world that God's way is the way that we have chosen for our life. That endorsement brings honor to God.

Beyond our actions, we are going to notice that it takes more than doing the right things to worship God. Our thoughts should bring glory to God. Great thoughts become a transformative way of thinking, which leads to real dedication to the Lord. How do we come to have the right thoughts that worship God? Well, as with basically everything, the Bible has something to say about that.

Ephesians 5:18
And do not get drunk with wine, for that is debauchery, but be filled with the Spirit…

Colossians 3:16
Let the word of Christ dwell in you richly…

The two above passages speak to what goes into your mind with two very different word pictures.

Instead of damaging your ability to reason and think clearly, be filled with the Spirit of God. I cannot help but think of a water pitcher. In order to distribute water, the pitcher has to have something in it. Metaphorically, the Spirit is the water that fills our pitcher. You can't think about something that you know nothing about. You must first learn about the thing that you hope to think about. Logically, that only makes sense. The Word of God is the Sword of the Spirit, in all its beauty. It is imperative to be filled with the Scriptures, because they are words that the Spirit guided the writers to record for us. Before we can worship God with our actions, our thoughts must come to see Him.

Did you catch the connection between spiritual things and physical things in Ephesians 5? The instruction is not to get drunk, but to be filled with the Spirit. Paul made a seamless transition from physical drunkenness to Spiritual fullness. When you become drunk, you damage your ability to glorify God with all of our subsequent actions, since you can't think about them with sobriety. The physical condition of your body can have damaging affects on your spiritual well-being. The state of your mind is something that you should worry about. Christians should be concerned about both things, as much as can be controlled.

The second image used to explain what controls your thoughts is one of dwelling. *"Let the word of Christ dwell in you richly."* The word of Christ can be explained two different ways, and they are both applicable. It can either be Jesus' words or the words about Jesus. There is no doubt that we should treasure the word of Jesus. Additionally, there is no question about whether or not we should value the story of Jesus. Both should dwell in us richly.

When someone lives with you, it is a dramatic experience. Usually, people don't haphazardly welcome other people into their home for long periods of time. It is a decision that we thoughtfully consider and pray about. If we let Christ dwell in us, it is a significant step in our lives. Christians should continually allow Christ's words to be a part of their life. When the Law was given to Moses, God told him to command the people to think about it when they rose and when they laid down. His Law should have been in their minds all the time.

Deuteronomy 6:6-9
And these words that I command you today shall be on your heart. You shall teach them diligently to your children, and shall talk of them when you sit in your house, and when you walk by the way, and when you lie down, and when you rise. You shall bind them as a sign on your hand, and they shall be as frontlets between your eyes. You shall write them on the doorposts of your house and on your gates.

Why should we expect things to be very different now? We shouldn't. We should constantly think about the words of the Bible, because they are our guide. When Paul wrote that they were to dwell with us, Scripture teaches a certain permanence with that command. Let it dwell with you. Take it with you wherever you go. Think about the words of Scripture when you're driving down the road. Think about the Bible when you're conversing with your spouse. Think about the wisdom in God's word when you're working. Let the word of Christ dwell in you!

To what length will you go to make money? There are times parents give up time with their kids. Your whole family may move across the globe for the right job. Ultimately, most of us give up at least forty hours a week to provide for our family. I'm not trying to point fingers with this exercise, but I am trying to point out how important taking care of our own is. How much more energy should we be willing to devote to make sure the word of Christ dwells in us? There is an added level to the indwelling of God's word. It should dwell in you richly. We will go to great lengths to make money, but are we willing to go to similar extents to cause the word of Christ to be in our thoughts constantly? We know the value of the word of God, but do our actions show that we think it is important to our families?

When we are filled with the Spirit, allowing the word of Christ to dwell in us richly, worship will naturally flow forth from us. As you would expect, both Ephesians 5 and Colossians 3 teach that very lesson.

Ephesians 5:18-20
And do not get drunk with wine, for that is debauchery, but be filled with the Spirit, addressing one another in psalms and hymns and spiritual

songs, singing and making melody to the Lord with your heart, giving thanks always and for everything to God the Father in the name of our Lord Jesus Christ.

Colossians 3:16
Let the word of Christ dwell in you richly, teaching and admonishing one another in all wisdom, singing psalms and hymns and spiritual songs, with thankfulness in your hearts to God.

Our worship to God is the organic overflow of the word of Christ being in our hearts. We need to examine what we let rule in our hearts. It is important that you have Christ's words in you, before you can share them with others. The instruction is to address one another in songs. How can you do that if you don't know any? How can you teach one another and advise one another, if you don't know what Christ said yourself? It appears from the passage that Paul thought the overflow of being filled with the Spirit was having spiritual things come out of your mouth in the form of songs.

When you look at the greater context of Ephesians 5, you recognize Paul was writing about their daily life. He wrote about sins they needed to uproot from their life. Plus, he talked about the attitude that they should have, which is to *"try to discern what is pleasing to the Lord" (Eph. 5:10)*. Colossians 3 is exactly the same way. He wrote about sin and the things they needed to leave behind, along with the things they needed to put on. These passages give credit to God for the great things in our lives. Our songs display our thankfulness to God for what He has done. The word of Christ should come out of us throughout the week, not just at an organized congregational event. Our Lord also addressed this issue by pointing to our hearts.

Matthew 12:34-35
You brood of vipers! How can you speak good, when you are evil? For out of the abundance of the heart the mouth speaks. The good person out of his good treasure brings forth good, and the evil person out of his evil treasure brings forth evil.

Whatever is in your heart will come out in your actions, speech, and your habits. If we have no good treasure in our heart, how can we expect to have good things to say? When we examine the Word of God daily, we can't help but talk about it. These thoughts, actions, and words bring honor to God. That is how we glorify God in all we do. We take Him, and His words, with us everywhere we go. We share the message of Jesus with those who do not know Him. We encourage Christians to keep the faith, trusting in the Lord each day. We live our lives to the glory of God. The resulting glory begins when we allow the word of Christ to dwell in us richly, by reading His word, and asking for His guidance.

The Hard Times

What happens when life gets challenging? There are times we may not feel like worshipping with our thoughts and actions. The devil is very good at throwing a lot at us at once. It can seem like the world is out to get us when we have multiple problems come to us. Well, the devil is trying to defeat you, but the hard times are the instances where we need to remember that God is there for us. We need to reach out to Him in prayer, because He is the answer to our problems.

There was a time that Paul and Silas were unjustly arrested. Paul cast a demon out of a servant girl, who made her master a great deal of money. When the master realized he could not make money from her anymore, he incited a mob to form against Paul and Silas. They were beaten with rods without a trial and thrown into prison. I can't really think of a bleaker scenario. They would have been bruised and bleeding. Their feet were fastened in the stocks. Before their arrest, they were teaching people about Jesus. Paul and Silas were in the middle of a good work that came to a screeching halt.

Are there ever times you don't understand what is going on with your life? You think you're doing the right things. You're serving God with all your heart. Despite your service, things still go wrong. You don't understand why you are being punished. When we think this way, we have missed the point. Good things and bad things come to all mankind. In fact, there are times that Christians face more difficulty because of the devil's opposition. We need to learn something from Paul and Silas. They were treated unfairly. As Roman citizens they deserved a trial, but they didn't get one. How did they respond?

Acts 16:25
About midnight Paul and Silas were praying and singing hymns to God, and the prisoners were listening to them

They were praying and singing in prison. That doesn't even make sense. *Or does it?* Consider some facts: Paul and Silas were still alive; those who suffer for the cause of Christ are blessed; no soldier could take away their eternal reward with God. We often have a choice to either focus on what is wrong with our life, or on what is going right in it. These two men decided to focus on what was great in their life. When you think about the blessings God has waiting for you, you want to sing and pray. Paul and Silas' reaction to their circumstances makes perfect sense when eternity was on their mind. I have good news for you. If you are in Christ, you have many of the same promises that Paul and Silas had. You can worship in the hard times of life. God can help you stand when everyone else is pushing you down. You can rejoice when everything is crashing around you. God is faithful. He will never leave you.

In addition to their perspective, there is another reason Paul and Silas worshipped in prison. They were in the inner portion of it. They knew that they were surrounded by other prisoners. The Bible made it clear that other prisoners were able to hear them. Winston Churchill once said, *"A pessimist sees the difficulty in every opportunity; an optimist sees the opportunity in every difficulty."* Instead of feeling sorry for themselves, Paul and Silas saw an opportunity. They were able to share their faith in God with the people around them. God was working in this situation. He unfastened their chains and opened the prison doors, through an earthquake. A guard was ready to kill himself because he thought the prisoners escaped. When Paul told them that they had not escaped, he asked them, *"Sirs, what must I do to be saved?" (Acts 16:30)* Paul instructs him to believe and his whole household was baptized into Christ. How do you think the soldier knew who to talk to about spiritual things? Their worship to God affected others. Other people were noticing how they responded to the worst of situations. How we suffer in this life will make an impact on other people. We may not think that other people are watching, but they are.

When we have an eternal perspective, we are not as worried about what happens to us in this life. We are concerned with how it affects eternity. That is weird to most people. It doesn't make sense to those who think only of this life. So many people look for peace and refuge in this life. When we clearly have peace of mind in the middle of loss, defeat, or trials, your peers will want what you have. That is when we point to the Lord, giving glory to Him for all He has done for you.

In addition to having an influence on others, worship in the hard times has an impact on you. Dr. David Schwartz wrote in *The Magic of Thinking Big*, *"Remember this: how you think when you lose determines how long it will be until you win."*[5] Wallowing in self-pity or grief does not help us grow. Yes, it is important to grieve for a time, but we can't stay in that state of mind. When we worship when we are down, we will not stay that way for long. As Dr. Schwartz said, how we handle the low points will dictate how many high points are on the horizon for us. Never forget this fact; God is faithful.

The Good Times

When life is difficult, the temptation is to look inward at how many things are going wrong. In a similar way, when life is at its best, we can look inward to give the credit. We deceive ourselves into thinking we accomplished all that we have done. We lead ourselves to believe that our success is something we can brag about. We may not say it, but arrogance is a real temptation when life is going in the right direction. Perhaps, we look down on people who are struggling in ways that we aren't at the moment. We may think we are better than others because we were recognized with an award or given a degree that your peers don't have.

One of the saddest things I have experienced in ministry is actually related to success. I have a friend who seems to have everything going for him: high paying job, good interpersonal skills, and unparalleled ambition. In spite of having everything, he felt empty. He did not know God. A Christian friend of mine and I tried to reach him, sharing the Gospel whenever we could, but to no avail. I pray that he will one day find the Lord. We, too, will feel empty if we find our success and happiness outside of the Lord.

The world measures success and a good life by wealth, status, and possessions. It is sad to say, but many who claim to be Christians define success in the same way. When we are happy with how much we have, we say our life is good. When we lack anything we want, our life isn't so good. Our hearts constantly ride a wave of what the oceans of life throw at us. That is in no way the life a Christian should live. God doesn't want our joy to be connected to our physical circumstances. He wants us to find our joy in Him, where there is lasting happiness and peace.

Jesus told a parable of a wealthy man, who had a particularly successful year (Luke 12:13-21). This man decided to tear down his barns to build bigger ones, to hold all of his stuff. He told himself he had plenty for many years and that he should relax. As the reader, we might assume this man had a good life. He planned to retire early and do whatever his heart desired. However, Jesus concluded the story with God's judgement against the man. God was going to take the rich man's life from him that night, because he was not rich toward God. Turns out, the rich man wasn't even going to be able to enjoy his abundant riches. Nothing is guaranteed in the physical realm, other than the fact that it does not last forever. Jesus told the story to warn his audience that their lives are more than what they have.

In times of prosperity, we cannot become confused over what matters in life. Living a life devoted to God and glorifying Him are still our greatest objectives. God is the one that allowed us to have the success that we are experiencing anyway. God gives good things to us, so we might worship Him.

There are real, substantive blessings that go along with living a life in thankfulness to God for what He has done. God has done things for you that are much more important than your salary. He has given you good things that are more valuable than any person in your life. He gave His only Son for you, so that you might be brought to a connection with Him. We have seen that an eternal perspective changes how we view the bad times, but it changes the good times too. Instead of congratulating ourselves for all that we have done, we give thanks to the One who actually gave us the tools to succeed. God opened the doors of opportunity for us, and put people in our life to bring about a favorable outcome.

Phil Robertson once said, *"I turned from my wicked ways and embraced Jesus. The next thing I knew, good times had come my way."* The good times in his life are anchored to his relationship with God, and not to the physical circumstances he is in. We should learn from that kind of faith.

If I have the right perspective on the blessings in my life, I can be all the more thankful. I thank God for my comfortable home, healthy family, and the sunshine that warms my face. God is good to us; He is good all the time. When thankfulness is constantly in our hearts, we are living the life of worship He intended. Thankfulness places God in the highest place, as the Eternal Source of our blessings.

Worthy

Above any command to worship God, we need to worship Him because He is worthy of all the praise and adoration. All of the hosts of Heaven spend eternity praising God as the One who is

Holy. In the book of Revelation, God showed John that everything in His Throne Room praises Him for who He is.

There are so many who have bought in to the notion that humans can know all there is to know about the universe. Human intellect has taken the place of God in the minds of many people. Instead of worship, scientific theories are on the lips of the average person today. I wonder if God looks down on us with sadness for the pride that we have. Mankind is arrogant regarding what they know and don't know. We can miss what is clearly in front of us when our heart is hard. In the path to finding conviction in the cross of Christ, we have to see that God and His ways are beyond our comprehension. A. W. Tozer, in his book on worship *The Purpose of Man*, confronted that point, *"We are the recipients of a grace meant to save us from self-centeredness and make worshippers out of us."*[6] God wants His people to take their focus off of themselves, so that we might see how Majestic He is. He saved us from ourselves with the hope that we might find Him. In wisdom, king David said, *"Delight yourself in the Lord, and He will give you the desires of your heart" (Psalm 37:4)*. When God is our delight and our song, we will always be satisfied.

I want to close this chapter by sharing a passage that describes God's greatness. Read these words with wonder and amazement. The same God that said these things loves you more than you can love Him; He deserves our worship.

Isaiah 40:12-17; 21-23; 28
Who has measured the waters in the hollow of His hand
and marked off the heavens with a span,
enclosed the dust of the earth in a measure
and weighed the mountains in scales
and the hills in a balance?

Who has measured the Spirit of the Lord,
or what man shows Him His counsel?
Whom did He consult,
and who made Him understand?
Who taught Him the path of justice,
and taught Him knowledge,
and showed Him the way of understanding?
Behold, the nations are like a drop from a bucket,
and are accounted as the dust on the scales;
behold, He takes up the coastlands like fine dust.
Lebanon would not suffice for fuel,
nor are its beasts enough for a burnt offering.
All the nations are as nothing before Him,
they are accounted by Him as less than nothing and emptiness.

Do you not know? Do you not hear?
Has it not been told you from the beginning?
Have you not understood from the foundations of the earth?
It is He who sits above the circle of the earth,
and its inhabitants are like grasshoppers;
who stretches out the heavens like a curtain,
and spreads them like a tent to dwell in;
who brings princes to nothing,
and makes the rulers of the earth as emptiness.

Have you not known? Have you not heard?
The Lord is the everlasting God,
the Creator of the ends of the earth.
He does not faint or grow weary;
His understanding is unsearchable.

Chapter 6

Fellowship

"Iron sharpens iron as one man sharpens another"
—Proverbs 27:17

Unless you are around Christians consistently, you likely don't hear the word fellowship very frequently. Fellowship is often used to describe church functions such as meals and Bible studies; or, it is used to represent spending time together. I, along with a number of Christians, don't fully explain the meaning of fellowship when we say that it is one of the events mentioned above. In fact, fellowship is much broader than the Christian usage. According to *A Greek-English Lexicon of the New Testament*, the Greek word for fellowship, *koinonia*, has the meaning, *"close association involving mutual interests and sharing."*[1] Regardless of affiliation, fellowship explains a connection between two entities. They are sharing time together for a common goal. In a secular usage, *koinonia* was used for business partners.[2]

The Greek verb is even utilized to explain that you should not be in fellowship with the wrong people.

1 Timothy 5:22
Do not be hasty in the laying on of hands, nor take part in the sins of others; keep yourself pure.

2 John 1:11
for whoever greets him takes part in his wicked works.

In the English Standard Version both verses have the words "take part" to define the verb in question. Paul and John represent two very different writing styles, yet they still both use fellowship to explain joining in others' sin. We all know it to be a fact of life that we are impacted by the people around us. It may be a small impact, but it is one nonetheless. Paul warned the Corinthians *"bad company ruins good morals" (1 Corinthians 15:33)*. We have a choice about who we surround ourselves with, and who we choose to spend time with. If we are influenced by the people around us, shouldn't we want to be around godly people? Shouldn't we want to fellowship with God himself? Is that even a Biblical concept? Believe it or not, the New Testament has a lot to say about fellowship.

God created all things in a perfect fashion. He looked at them and called them good. If God viewed them as good, there was no fault in them. The first people, Adam and Eve, sinned against the command God handed to them, thus introducing sin into the world. From that moment, sin has separated mankind from God. This separation was no mere creek that could be waded across. Our sins created an impassable divide that doomed mankind to eternal separation from God. That is, until Jesus bridged the gap by taking the sins of the world on the cross. His sacrifice and subsequent exaltation, brought about a new age, where mankind can have a relationship with God. Paul painted this beautiful image through his discussions on reconciliation. He wrote in a few places about how we have been reconciled to God, through Jesus. In other words, we have been brought back to God. We now have hope and a future with God, through Christ. Jesus gives us the opportunity to be in fellowship with God.

New Relationship

A close examination of the Old Testament reveals a different kind of relationship between God and His people. In the Greek Old Testament (LXX), the word *koinonia* is not used of the relationship between God and mankind, only man (woman) to man (woman) relationships. That is astounding! Under the Old Law, mankind had a legal and covenantal relationship with God. While those could be used to explain the Christian age, they are only part of the picture. Because of the blood of Jesus, we can have fellowship with God. For literally thousands of years, people were not able to have the special relationship with God that you can have. When I researched this topic, I couldn't help but come to worship God for this wonderful gift. God has been so good to us, even though we deserved none of His goodness. J. I. Packer in his book *Knowing God* expressed this gratitude, *"There is, however, equally great incentive to worship and love God in the thought that, for some unfathomable reason, he wants me as his friend, and desires to be my friend, and has given his Son to die for me in order to realize this purpose."*[3] God loves the seemingly unloveable sinner that I am, and He wants to be in fellowship with me. Praise be to God!

There are some things we should know about what our fellowship with God will look like. The apostle John taught us in 1 John 1 that God is light, and there is no darkness in Him at all. Christians must affirm the greatest and otherness of God. He is so much greater than anything on this earth. Many times God judged the peoples for worshipping created things instead of worshipping Him, the Uncreated One. God is so great that He warrants constant praise from the angelic beings of Heaven. They are constantly praising Him. They shout *"Holy, Holy, Holy is the Lord God Almighty" (Revelation 4:8)*. Paul described God as One who dwelt in unapproachable light (1 Timothy 6:16). God transcends our very understanding. A. W. Tozer wrote in *The Knowledge of the Holy*, *"Man for all his genius is but an echo of the original Voice, a reflection of the uncreated Light."*[4] No matter how much mankind might achieve, it pales in comparison to what God has already done. Human greatness is simply the constructive use of what God has granted mankind to accomplish.

In light of God's greatness, we must admit to our frailty and sin. John wrote that we cannot deny our sinfulness. When we do so, John said we make God a liar. May this never be! In order to remain in fellowship with God, we have to confess our sins. God does not accept pride toward Him. Humility should define us. If we are in fellowship with God, it is because of His mercy and grace—not our own accolades. Our response to God is in a humble honesty toward Him, regarding who we are. When we come to Him in this fashion, we can receive His goodness. We can be in His fellowship. In our arrogance we are detestable in God's sight.

John wrote about what it took to be in fellowship with God. The instruction is to walk in the light as He is in the light (1 John 1:7). The Light of God is where the blood of Jesus will wash us from our sins. What does it mean to walk in the light? From John's writings the answer is apparent—love God and love others. When we show this love toward God and our fellow man, we are acting like the Light, which is God, who is Love. Walking in the light also includes a confession of the sins that we have committed and repenting of them.

I have always thought of a two lane road to describe what it is like to walk in the light. There is a center yellow line that runs down the middle with two paved sections on either side of it. It is abundantly clear from Scripture that God is the light, and we are mere reflections of His brilliance. We aren't perfect in the way that He is. Our responsibility is to remain as close to the Light as possible. We have to remain in His protection. Light has an area of influence that can illuminate the path ahead. The lanes on the road act as an example to show us that there is an area nearest to God that has His Presence. There is a point where we enter the darkness, when we wander too far away from the light. When you are driving, safety is found on the road; in the same way, we are safe in the place where the light is still visible. Some wish to compare walking in the light to flipping a light switch. You're saved one moment in God's presence and the next you are nowhere near Him. That teaching is incongruent with John's teachings on the subject. John wrote that you need to confess your sins to receive forgiveness from God. Additionally, he wrote that we needed to admit that we have sin in order to receive forgiveness from the Lord.

Perhaps another example from the Scriptures will help to explain our fellowship with God. He adopted us as sons and daughters of God, the Father (Romans 8). How many times have you failed your parents? Parents, how many times will you forgive your children? Most parents would do everything in their power to help their children to succeed. They will endure repeated abuse of trust and mistreatment before they even consider closing communication. We are more patient with our own flesh and blood than we are with anyone else. Shouldn't our adoption into God's family mean something? It means everything! To break fellowship with God, we have to commit repeated willful sin. As long as we want to be in His family, walk in humility toward Him, and follow His direction, we will enjoy the benefits of His Presence.

The blood of Jesus allows us to be in fellowship with God. Human perfection cannot give us this ability, because none of us are innocent before God. As we are walking in the light, we will sin; but, we have to confess our sin and ask for forgiveness. We should be aware that there is a point when we leave the light. If we look to Jesus daily and fellowship with God, through the Spirit, we won't have to worry about how close we come to the darkness. We will be led by God in such a way that sin loses its power over our lives. We will have moments of weakness, but they will be the exception rather than the norm. John wrote to assure his audience of the confidence that Christians should have in their salvation. He had no intentions of muddying the waters through his explanation of walking in the light. John gives us confidence that if we walk close to the Light and confess our sins, there will be forgiveness found in Jesus.

Remembrance

God, in His infinite wisdom, knew that we would easily forget all that He has done for us through Christ. That is one reason Jesus gave us an opportunity to share in his death each week. Jesus set in motion a Supper that would commemorate his death on the cross. When we partake of the Lord's Supper, we are remembering the body and blood of Christ.

We have monuments to numerous key figures in history, because they were pivotal in bringing about victory, liberation, or justice. Not only that, but we have national symbols that invoke patriotism and pride in our country. God set aside days of remembrance, monuments, and special meals to remember what

He had done for them. Jesus' institution of the Lord's Supper is important because when we partake, we shift our focus away from ourselves on to what his sacrifice means for our lives. Consider the following verses that recount the night the Supper was instituted.

Matthew 26:26-29
Now as they were eating, Jesus took bread, and after blessing it broke it and gave it to the disciples, and said, "Take, eat; this is my body." And he took a cup, and when he had given thanks he gave it to them, saying, "Drink of it, all of you, for this is my blood of the covenant, which is poured out for many for the forgiveness of sins. I tell you I will not drink again of this fruit of the vine until that day when I drink it new with you in my Father's kingdom."

Jesus wanted his disciples to remember the depth of his love for them. It is no different for us today. When we partake, we remember that Jesus gave his entire life so that we might live. We commemorate the blood that was shed so that we can be in fellowship with God. There is no possible way to be in fellowship with God apart from Jesus Christ. Every time we remember Jesus' sacrifice we are filled with gratitude and humility before God. His grace and mercy allows us to have a deep relationship with our Creator.

We have further teachings concerning the Lord's Supper. The Corinthian church had perverted the Supper. They were making an entire meal out of it and using it to broaden the socioeconomic gap within the congregation. In that day and time there was a large disparity between the rich and the poor. The Corinthians were well known for being wealthy, but not all Christians were rich. There were some who did not have enough to eat. When they were eating the Lord's Supper, some had a full meal, others had nothing, yet another group got drunk. Their wrongdoing was rooted in selfishness. They had turned what was supposed to be the Lord's Supper into the Corinthian Supper. It was about showing off what they had to eat, and indulging their own flesh. They didn't even wait for each other. The Lord was no longer a part of that supper. Instead, they flaunted what they had to make other brothers in Christ feel less valuable than they were.

To our benefit, Paul had to explain to the Corinthians what the Lord's supper was all about—the Lord. We should examine ourselves in light of the body and blood of Christ. The Church needs to remember each element of his sacrifice. He mentioned, within his commands concerning the Supper, that when we take part in the Lord's Supper, we are proclaiming the Lord's death until he comes. Remembering the Lord is also about being a beacon to the rest of the world. We carry the banner of his body and blood, which gives us fellowship with God.

There's something special here that we have failed to mention. In addition to remembering Jesus' sacrifice, we get to share in the body and blood of Christ. Paul will go so far as to say that when we partake of the Lord's Supper, we fellowship with the body and blood of Christ. We are joined together with God by what Jesus did for us. Plus, from 1 Corinthians 10, we see that we partake of the same bread. In other words, we are united by what Jesus did for us. The Lord's Supper is the point in which our fellowship with God and our fellowship with each other collides. I am in a relationship with God, so I will observe the Lord's supper to remember what He did for me. You are in a relationship with God, which leads you to partake of the Lord's Supper. We are made one at the foot of the cross; there is unity in what Jesus did. Those who are in Christ are in him together.

One Another

Spending time with fellow Christians was probably the first example of fellowship that came to mind, but, as we have seen, our fellowship with God leads us into a union with other Christians. Our worship on the first day of the week, which contains the Lord's Supper, is a time of fellowship. We share in our worship of God. The Church is the primary institution where Christian fellowship takes place. The Lord adds us to the body of Christ when we are baptized (1 Corinthians 12:13). Our connection with each other is a design from the mind of the Lord.

The early Church was constantly committed to one another. So many of their activities could be described as fellowship.

Acts 2:42-47 parts omitted
And they devoted themselves to the apostles' teaching and the fellowship, to the breaking of bread and the prayers…And all who believed were together and had all things in common…And day by day, attending the temple together and breaking bread in their homes…praising God and having favor with all the people. And the Lord added to their number day by day those who were being saved.

The amount of time the first century Church spent together would likely dwarf whatever small amount of time our congregations spend together. I've often heard lessons that use this passage to champion doctrinal purity and the need to partake of the Lord's Supper, but rarely do I hear it used to promote spending a large portion of our time in Christian fellowship. They often broke bread in their homes. They attended the temple day by day. It seems there were more days they spent with Christians than days they did not. When was the last time you had others in your home to share a meal? How many days a week do you share time with fellow believers?

Consider the first century setting of Acts 2. The Church owned no buildings that we know of. They met in each other's homes. They used public places to meet together for fellowship, such as the temple. We would think the early churches were at a disadvantage for not owning a large place to worship, yet they were seemingly always together. Conversely, the majority of churches in America own or rent a building. How many of our church buildings lie dark and dormant five or six days a week? We spend thousands, sometimes millions, of dollars on a facility that is largely neglected. I don't think we should get rid of our buildings, quite the opposite. I think we should *use* them. A church building that is humming with activity is likely a growing church. Bible studies, community events, and other times of fellowship should characterize our local churches. In addition to the section in Acts 2, consider the following passages:

Acts 5:42
And every day, in the temple and from house to house, they did not cease teaching and preaching that the Christ is Jesus.

Acts 17:11
Now these Jews were more noble than those in Thessalonica; they received the word with all eagerness, examining the Scriptures daily to see if these things were so.

They loved the Lord and loved sharing time in God's word together. The early Church was committed to daily fellowship. We would do well to follow their example by looking for more opportunities to fellowship in Christ.

The basis for the Church's commitment to fellowship is found in the two great commandments—love God and love our neighbor. Loving God leads me to worship and study His Word consistently. Loving my neighbor inspires me to help my neighbor go to Heaven. How can we help the other members of the Church go to Heaven when we never spend time with them? How can I help lighten your load if I don't know what you are struggling with? How can I encourage you if I don't know your insecurities? There are so many biblical commands that are left unfollowed when the Church's members are isolated. Dedication to God and mankind are realized through fellowship.

In *The Other 80 Percent* Thumma and Bird polled church members regarding their connection to the local congregation. One member had this to say:

"I realized that I could not describe what makes our church unique, what it stands for. I do not have close friends in the church at this time and I think that all makes a big difference in my regular attendance, regardless of time, distance and health."[5]

This person's attendance was damaged, because of the lack of relationships they had at a congregation. They had a dim view of the Church's vision, which was likely not their fault. This member was willing to disregard time, distance, and health, as long as she was closely connected to the membership. Have you ever been in that situation? Likely, you have been in that scenario multiple times. From this example, we realize the importance of healthy Christian fellowship. That is why Jesus, as well as the other New Testament teachers, spoke so often about the need to treat mankind with respect, love, and kindness.

Christians can have a damaging effect on the Church when they don't act like Christ. C. S. Lewis wrote in *Mere Christianity*, *"When we Christians behave badly, or fail to behave well, we are making Christianity unbelievable to the outside world."*[6] Our influence in the community can take a hit when our congregations don't act like Christ. The opposite is also true. When our church shows love for one another, spends time together, and genuinely worships God, the world will take notice. Our world has never been more connected, but we are still isolated and lonely. Humans crave the connections the Church has within itself. When guests come into our assemblies, do they see a church committed to fellowship?

The Need For Christian Fellowship

It shouldn't surprise us that our surroundings make a large impact on our development. You could take two fish of the same species, put them in different environments, and you will end up with vastly different results. Water quality, diet, predation, and the size of body of water will each affect the development of those fish. Likewise, who and what we surround ourselves with makes a great deal of difference in what we become. Influences take their toll as time goes on.

If I asked you about how you would want your child to grow up, what would you say? You would want them to be with good kids, who would be a good influence on them. You would want them to go to the best schools, so they would get the best education. You would want them to have hobbies and develop good skills. When they graduate high school, you would want them to be on a path to finding a good career to support their own family.

There are clear, good answers to the questions concerning our children. We would have no problem with coming up with a decent path for them. It is because we have thought about what it takes to succeed in the world in which we live. We have gone through the development that they are going through. We've made mistakes and found success in different areas. Have we considered a path for spiritual development in the same way we have thought about their physical growth? Do we even consider our own spiritual development? If we are experiencing a lack of growth, it could be attributed to a lack of intentionality. Goal-oriented thinking causes you to make a plan. Laying out steps will allow you to achieve your goal one step at a time. Essentially, that is the way you have organized your life. In order to grow spiritually, you have to lay out steps to reach maturity.

Growing in Christ involves the things we have studied to this point—power, learning, love, faith, and worship. A step that can easily be overlooked is fellowship. To open the chapter we read, *"Iron sharpens iron as one man sharpens another"* (Proverbs 27:17). One of the major reasons the Church exists is to strengthen individual Christians. We need each other to get to Heaven. We have to *"bear one another's burdens"* (Galatians 6:2). We have to encourage each other. However, your church could be holding you back. Your church could be stunting your growth, in the same way a deficient school system could. Your church could be so big that you can't use your gifts of leadership or service. Are you able to grow and help others to grow where you worship consistently?

Churches have their own culture. There is a certain attitude toward study, worship, and growth that can be felt over time. An outsider can spend a few months, if not less time, with a new congregation and understand the direction of that church. There will be exceptions, but the majority of members will conform to

113

that congregation's attitude. Culture within a church influences our growth, or lack thereof, in Christ. So much of the burden of culture falls on leadership. Inadequate leaders will lead the congregation in the wrong direction. Good leaders will encourage growth and point everyone to Christ, the ultimate Leader. If you aren't happy with your church's leadership, don't give up on that church. Be the leader they need or help others to be better leaders. As a minister, there are people I rely on for encouragement and teaching. They give me wisdom to handle situations that arise. Your leaders need the same sort of wisdom and encouragement. Let's look in the mirror at our churches and see what kind of environment they are.

Study

Do church leaders point to God's Word for the source of their motivation and decision making?

Are Bible studies well-attended at your congregation?

Do members sigh in frustration over the opportunity to 'dig deeper?'

Each of the answers to these questions will say something different about how your church approaches study. What we see in the book of Acts is a church that meets day by day, to study the Word of God. They were excited to dig deep into the Scriptures to find allusions to Christ. They were commended and praised for searching the Scriptures daily.

Studying the Bible is essential for Christian growth and direction. It is a *"lamp to my feet and a light to my path" (Psalm 119:105)*. The Word of God is from the very breath of God, and is useful for so many things such as teaching and correction (2 Timothy 3:16-17). J. I. Packer wrote, *"Disregard the study of God, and you sentence yourself to stumble and blunder through life blindfolded, as it were, with no sense of direction and no understanding of what surrounds you."*[7] Our churches have to be led by the Word of God. If we are not committed to letting it lead us, we are fumbling through this life without a direction. If you or your church isn't growing, perhaps study needs to take a more prominent role.

Worship

Would you characterize your church as 'going through the motions' when you gather for worship?

Does everyone participate in the worship or does everyone watch a select few?

Is it common for worshippers to get emotional? (crying, smiling, or surprise)

Does it seem like leaders try to speed through parts of worship?

One of the biggest issues Jesus had with the religious leaders, of his day, was they worshipped God without their heart. They had all the right sacrifices; but, they didn't think about the meaning or purpose. They were hypocritical. Worship should have elements of spontaneity. When they have the same order for years, it is easy to become mechanical. I'm not suggesting we change everything, but some change from time to time is healthy. Change the number of songs, length of lessons, and the order every now and again.

If you're having an issue with participation, have pointed conversations with members who are neglecting to be engaged. The Biblical command is to sing. The whole church should be a part of that. When we all are actively engaged in worship, emotions will come. Tears can follow singing about the sacrifice of Christ. Smiles should be seen when we remember that home in Heaven that waits for us.

Growth

Would you or your fellow church members be happy if your church had the same number of members in 10 years?

When was the last time someone from the community was baptized into Christ?

Do your leaders make statements like, "That is just the way we have always done it" to give a reason for future activity?

Why do you many churches stay the same over long periods of time? The congregation has the wrong attitude toward growth. Jesus said to go and make disciples of all nations (Matthew 28:18-20 & Mark 16:15-16). How can you follow that command and still want things to stay the same? You can't! A commitment to God from the Church is a commitment to growth. Paul outlined the process when he stated, *"I planted, Apollos watered, but God gave the growth" (1 Corinthians 3:6)*. If we are planting and watering seeds constantly, God will give growth.

Practically speaking, we need to be changing our approach on a consistent basis. This is not a change of Biblical doctrine, but it is change on how we deliver it. Nowadays, the internet should be a tool your church is actively using. Visitors will look at your website before they will visit. It is their first contact with you. Preachers should preach relevant messages. Paul preached to the Greeks using their proverbs and sayings. Peter preached to the Jews with the Old Testament because it was what they were familiar with. Today, we should use current events, modern books, and applicable anecdotes to explain the message of Christ. They do not change the message, but allow it to be easier to understand.

Results

How is your church doing? More often than not, your church's mindset will become your mindset. How the people closest to you feel about study, worship, and growth will become how you feel about those things. If there is a deficiency, be the first domino to bring about positive change at your church. Hold your leaders accountable for the direction in which they are leading you. We all need good, Christian fellowship to grow in our walk with God. Asking these questions is a way of evaluating what kind of fellowship you are receiving. We are all working together to go to be with God for eternity.

Ephesians 4:15-16
Rather, speaking the truth in love, we are to grow up in every way into him who is the head, into Christ, from whom the whole body, joined and held together by every joint with which it is equipped, when each part is working properly, makes the body grow so that it builds itself up in love.

Who Did Jesus Fellowship With?

In all things we look to Christ as our example. We can learn something from how he handled who he spent time with. Jesus rubbed elbows with the religious elite and the wealthy, traveled with the twelve, and ate with the prostitutes and sinners. He really didn't avoid anyone. He was willing to help and influence everyone he met.

117

I think there is a lesson here for us. We are not able to be around Christians all the time, and we shouldn't look to just be with Christians. We still have to try to reach the lost of this world. We need to remain connected to those in the world so that we can give them the Gospel. In whatever situation we find ourselves in, we need to look to be the light of the world. Jesus came to save sinners and help the needy. When we take the name of Christ wherever we go, we can be like him toward people who need him the most.

Chapter 7

Repeat

"Discipline without direction is drudgery." —*Donald Whitney*[1]

Come on, why do I have to do that? Why do I need to clean the house? Why do I need to go to work today? We all have objections to activities we need to do in this life. It can be frustrating to have to do these seemingly meaningless activities over and over again. If it isn't physical things it is the spiritual. Why do I need to read? Why do I need to pray? Why do I need to practice relying on God? I have thought and heard these very things. I would imagine that you have too.

You could categorize activities such as reading, praying, serving, and giving as disciplines. When those disciplines are for spiritual betterment they become spiritual disciplines. Simply put, you discipline your body for a time to receive a spiritual reward. Some of the rewards are immediate; but, most of the time we don't reap the rewards until after years of implementation. Donald Whitney claimed that God uses three major catalysts to bring about change in our life: other people, our circumstances, and the spiritual disciplines. Whitney points out in his book *Spiritual Disciplines For The Christian Life* that the spiritual disciplines are the only one of the three that we have control over. God uses our efforts to bless us and to help us to become like Jesus.[1]

Change

It is also important to realize that your habits can change. A large portion of people have bought into the lie that you cannot change. We pass along the idiom, *"You can't teach an old dog new tricks"* to our own detriment. There is actual brain science that supports the concept of our mind having the ability to change. Neuroplasticity is the *"capacity of neurons and neural networks in the brain to change their connections and behaviour in response to new information, sensory stimulation, development, damage, or dysfunction."*[2] Our brains are changing over time, as a result of the stimuli we are putting them in contact with.

The type of neuroplasticity that pertains to our study is known as map expansion.[2] When we learn new skills, our brain is fundamentally changing to develop the new skill. That is why skilled artists, musicians, or athletes are able to do incredibly complex actions with little or no conscious thought. They have trained their brains in such a way that something difficult becomes natural.

Consider how neuroplasticity can impact you as a Christian. There is brain science to support the fact that your mind can change through repetition. In addition to the power of the Holy Spirit, God has made you in such a way that you can change when you constantly come in contact with spiritual things. We can see positive results from exercising our minds. Praise God we can change!

Reward

I want to clarify what I mean when I use the word reward. I don't mean work (discipline) so that you may receive what God owes you. Instead, Jesus and the early Christians saw it differently. They disciplined themselves to be ready for the difficulties that awaited them, to reconnect with God, or as an act of gratitude for what the Lord had done for them. The rewards were spiritual in nature and they were blessed with the ability to endure hardship. Our mindset toward the disciplines and activities of the Christian life needs to change. Our motives should be like those of Jesus. Our desires should be patterned after the desires of Christ, when humanly possible.

Going back to our original thought, we have heard or asked the question, "Why?" While it is not a bad question to ask, we have looked away from our purpose. Our focus is on how difficult the task currently is, or how hard it will become. We have to refocus our attention back to what the goal is. Ultimately, we have the goal of glorifying God and living with Him forever in eternity. We're trying to get somewhere. Along the way we need to grow in our walk with God, which will involve discipline. When we lose sight of the goal, as Whitney pointed out, the hard work becomes drudgery.

Goals

Now, let's zoom in on a smaller level. There are goals that every Christian can agree on. We'll look at one specific one here—you know you should read your Bible more. God's Word is clear about how important it is to the life of the Christian.

2 Timothy 3:16-17
All Scripture is breathed out by God and profitable for teaching, for reproof, for correction, and for training in righteousness, that the man of God may be complete, equipped for every good work.

Psalm 119:105
Your word is a lamp to my feet and a light to my path.

     No matter how much you study it, there is more to learn. We feel a certain amount of pressure to know more than we do now. Don't let that pressure scare you away. I am confident that you can become a good Bible student. First, set a specific goal. Set the goal of reading for ten minutes every day or to read one chapter each day. Setting a specific goal gives you a concrete checkpoint to follow. If you set the goal of reading more each day, you will never actually know if you reach it; but, a specific goal will have specific results. You either meet it or you don't. Make sure your goal is attainable though. There are few worse feelings than failure. If you need to, set your original goal of reading one verse every day. Whatever you do, make sure your initial goal is manageable. Set yourself up to succeed.

     Try your first goal for a couple of weeks. Modify it as it suits your schedule. By this point you will have developed a Bible studying habit; and, you will likely have the desire to read more or cover more ground each day. Don't think too far beyond what you're doing, unless this form of goal setting has been very easy for you. We can become overwhelmed if we try goals that are too large. Reading the entire Bible may be a long term goal but don't think of that initially. After all, as the ancient proverb of Laozi says, *"The journey of a thousand miles begins with a single step."* Take a step each day to ensure that you make it to your destination.

Crossway, the nonprofit publishing ministry, determined how long it would take to read the Bible. According to their research, in order to read the entire Bible in one year you would only need to read 12 minutes a day.[3] *12 minutes.* Most books of the Bible can be read in a half hour or less. How much time do you spend on social media? I know I spend at least an hour every day on it. How much time do you spend reading other things? How much time do spend watching TV? Wouldn't we be better off devoting more time to God's word and cutting back just a little on some extra activities?

You can do that. You can read a small portion each day to achieve a lifelong goal. This goal-setting practice can be applied to most anything in life. Set small, manageable "steps" to get to where you want to go. I cannot give a high enough recommendation to *Your Best Year Ever* by Michael Hyatt.[4] He dives deeply into goal setting which can be modified to fit spiritual goals.

This book you are reading is a culmination of months of single steps. On days I didn't want to write I would set a goal of 250 words, which is basically a paragraph. Often times, I would crank out way more; once I started, I couldn't seem to stop writing.

Some goal-setting experts break it down even further. Some will say read one word, then you'll read a second, a third, before you know it you've read a few pages. A few pages of reading a day can tackle the most daunting books. I think this chapter is one of the most exciting in this book for me because I have benefitted most from it. God has used the goals that I have set to transform my life. This is the beauty of the spiritual disciplines. When you repeat a good activity, it develops into a part of your character.

Another goal that I have, is to read one book a month. After two years I have read over forty books. To some, that isn't much but to someone who used to despise reading, it is huge. It was manageable enough that I knew I could do it. It was also more than I was doing, so it stretched me. Reading a book a month has exposed me to Biblical teaching on a variety of subjects such as holiness, God's character, love, and how the Bible has been passed down to us. Secular topics those books covered were beneficial as well. Since it was a manageable goal, I have been able to achieve it at least 24 times in a row. You can have the same sort of results too. Keep the goal in mind.

When you begin to think about the goal rather than the work it takes to get there, you will begin to enjoy what you are doing. Malcolm Gladwell wrote in an excellent book, *Outliers* "*Hard work is a prison sentence only if it does not have meaning.*"[5] I'm sure there are some of you that can relate to this. If you love your job, it doesn't always feel like work. Most of the time you enjoy what it takes to do what you do. Even if you have to do something you don't like, you know why you have to do it. It isn't prison when you know and can see the benefits of the work. Now that I have seen the meaning and benefit of reading, I don't feel imprisoned to have to read a book. You can experience this sort of liberation too. You can find meaning and blessings in the spiritual disciplines in which you need to grow.

On top of any other goal we might have, we need to fix our eyes on eternity. The Preacher, in Ecclesiastes, wrote that God put eternity in man's hearts (Ecclesiastes 3:11). Paul wrote that the Christian's citizenship is in Heaven. The spiritual disciplines are so important, because they contribute to the much larger goal of glorifying God into eternity. In order to get there, we have to grow here on this earth. God uses these disciplines to work upon our hearts which causes us to grow stronger. God blesses us each and every step of the way, when we are focusing on Him.

Notice a sad truth from the earlier quote from Malcolm Gladwell—"*Hard work is a prison sentence only if it does not have meaning.*"[5] If you don't know the reason for what you are doing, you are handed a prison sentence. Discipline is hard work. Repeating something, over and over again, isn't easy. The obvious conclusion is we must know why we are disciplining ourselves in order that we might find joy in doing it. Let's dive deep into what Jesus and the early disciples said about our habits. They disciplined themselves to be ready for the difficulties that awaited them, to reconnect with God, or as an act of gratitude for what the Lord had done for them.

Preparation

1 Timothy 4:6-10
If you put these things before the brothers, you will be a good servant of Christ Jesus, being trained in the words of the faith and of the good doctrine that you have followed. Have nothing to do with irreverent, silly myths. Rather train yourself for godliness; for while bodily training is of some value, godliness is of value in every way, as it holds promise for the present life and also for the life to come. The saying is trustworthy and deserving of full acceptance. For to this end we toil and strive, because we have our hope set on the living God, who is the Savior of all people, especially of those who believe.

The apostle Paul instructed Timothy, his son in the faith. He wanted to make sure he knew what sort of training was most important. Paul wanted him to remain committed to the truth, to avoid foolish controversies, and to train himself for godliness. Not only that, notice the words used to describe how the Christian should aim to reach heaven—toil and strive. The words train, toil, and strive imply that our goals will be reached through hard work. Salvation, through Christ, is a free gift; but, the Christian life is challenging. Goals like godliness require training. Toil and striving are needed to reach the life that is to come.

The first reason we will consider for discipline is preparation. We are working toward a goal in mind. Paul told Timothy to train with godliness as the desired result. What does that training entail? Consider what else Paul told his son in the faith:

Selected from 1 Timothy 4:11-16
Command and teach these things…set the believers an example in speech, in conduct, in love, in faith, in purity…devote yourself to the public reading of Scripture, to exhortation, to teaching…Practice these things, immerse yourself in them, so that all may see your progress. Keep a close watch on yourself and on the teaching. Persist in this, for by so doing you will save both yourself and your hearers.

This isn't intended to be an exhaustive list, but it is a good start. We see Scripture reading, example setting, and consistency as highlights from Paul's instruction. Through godliness we reveal God to the world, in the same way Christians should be the light. We are not the light, God is, but we are reflecting it in such a way that God receives glory for our example. We search the Scriptures and practice implementing them so that we resemble Christ. This is at the heart of Christianity.

Training involves repetition. Many have said things like, *"Repetition is the mother of learning."* My Ohio Valley University professor, Dr. Terry, was one of them. I can't tell you how many times he said it. He was right though. When you repeat something, over and over again, it becomes a learned habit or skill. Once we center our habits on growing in our walk with God, our life becomes an upward path toward Heaven. We will grow closer to God each day. More and more we learn what it takes to become pleasing to God, which allows us to handle each day better than we did the one previous.

We want to act better, but we will get the same results until something changes. Our practice is only as good as the types of exercises we are performing. If we practice failing, we will get better at failing. Instead, go about it in a different way. Replace the sin with a habit of God-centered thinking. Pray to God and ask Him for help. Additionally, a change in our action has to begin with a change in our thinking. Filling our minds with godly things will help us to be more godly. To train ourselves for godliness requires us to become acquainted with godly things. We know that God's Word has been preserved for us, and we know that His people are striving for same things. Spending time in the Word will change your thoughts, because it is God-breathed. God's Spirit is speaking to us through words left for us. The early church knew this, which is why we read about them spending time together focused on godly things. To act more Christ-like takes preparation. We discipline ourselves to be prepared for the flaming darts of the evil one.

Also, we need to be prepared for the questions that arise. Peter admonished early Christians to *"always being prepared to make a defense to anyone who asks you for a reason for the hope that is in you" (1 Peter 3:15)*. Christians should equip themselves for the storms of this life, and questioning from outsiders.

Have you ever been unprepared in a Bible study? There have been times that I have been underprepared for sermons and it is a feeling that you don't soon forget. If anger, embarrassment, and frustration were thrown in a blender, you would get a word that explains what it feels like. I never want to feel that way again. It drives me to study deeper and commit more time to preparation. Souls are affected when we don't have words from God. Our preparation allows us to be in tune with what the Spirit has laid out for us in His word.

Consider for a moment how often the early Christians would study with Jews and Pagans. They had to have a knowledge of their own faith, plus the beliefs of the other person. Peter quoted Old Testament Scriptures and Paul quoted philosophers to reach their audience. Don't you think that kind of knowledge took a while to acquire?

Every Christian should have a thorough knowledge of what it takes to become a Christian, the basic teachings of Jesus, and the church. If you don't have that now, you now have a goal to set for yourself. Find out what you do not know, and learn it. It will take discipline, but you should do it so you have an answer for those that ask about the hope that is within you. We need to know these things for our own faith, but we also need to know so we can teach others.

Connection

The most important reason anyone would discipline themselves is to connect with the Lord. There is no greater pursuit given to mankind than to strive to be with their Maker. If you need a reason to read your Bible, pray, fast, serve, or meditate, here it is. When we do these things, we are able to draw nearer to God. Jesus exemplified this while he was on the earth.

During Jesus' ministry the crowds loved him. He was their hospital, meal ticket, and entertainment. It was a challenge for him to go anywhere without drawing a large crowd. There were times

Jesus had to walk away from those crowds so that he could pray to God. Many times we read of Jesus going to a quiet place to pray. Consider the following:

Luke 5:16
But he would withdraw to desolate places and pray.

Matthew 14:23a
And after he had dismissed the crowds, he went up on the mountain by himself to pray.

Mark 1:35
And rising very early in the morning, while it was still dark, he departed and went out to a desolate place, and there he prayed.

Wait a minute. Wasn't Jesus perfect? What sins did he need to ask forgiveness for? Wasn't Jesus able to heal? What healing did he need from God? The reasons we pray to God don't seem to line up with what Jesus would have needed. Jesus needed to be connected to his Father. Jesus was the most disciplined man that has ever walked the face of the earth. He would leave the adulation and praise to go be alone with God. There were even times he rose early in the morning or stayed up late, because he knew it was the only time he could be alone with his Father.

If the Son of God needed to spend time alone in prayer, how can we claim to have a relationship with God without it? We need to be connected to God every day. How can we expect to get through this life without repeated discipline? Jesus never complained about this time with his Father; instead, he seemed to crave it. According to John 1, Jesus was in the beginning with God.

He knows what it is like to be in God's glorious presence. We would do well to desire time connected to our Father.

Find a quiet place to meditate and pray. Jesus commanded the early disciples to go to their room and shut the door to pray. It is meant to be private. I have always found a mountain side to be a good place. Your office may be quiet enough to focus on the Lord. Wherever you find, make sure your connection to God is on your mind. We can be guilty of treating God like our genie. Don't forget that your fellowship with God is a unique blessing for Christians. God has been good to us.

In addition to connecting with God through prayer and Word reading, I want us to focus on Hebrews 12:1-2.

Hebrews 12:1-2
Therefore, since we are surrounded by so great a cloud of witnesses, let us also lay aside every weight, and sin which clings so closely, and let us run with endurance the race that is set before us, looking to Jesus, the founder and perfecter of our faith, who for the joy that was set before him endured the cross, despising the shame, and is seated at the right hand of the throne of God.

In the hustle and bustle of life our focus needs to be on Christ. Our responsibility is to lay aside the sins in our life and run behind Jesus. Laying aside sin is a battle we are waging our whole lives. Thanks be to God Jesus paid the price for our sins and His mercies cover our sins! Our goal is holiness which requires a fixation on the perfect man, Jesus.

This sort of focus is another goal of the spiritual disciplines. I can't focus on Jesus of whom I've never heard, prayed through, or sacrificed for. The disciplines teach us about Christ and how he would have us to live. Also, we are to run with endurance.

Endurance can be extremely challenging. There is a reason we don't give up. Namely, the fact that Jesus didn't give up on us. He endured the cross and took the pain for our sins. Jesus' endurance leads us into the last motivation we will consider for repeated focus on God and His work.

Gratitude

Christians endure and discipline themselves out of gratitude for what Jesus has done for us. At the core of this book is the cross of Jesus Christ. Jesus' sacrifice is the center of the Gospel. The Good News is the fact we have an opportunity to be with the Lord. The broken relationship between God and mankind has been mended, by the blood of Jesus. I can't think about the Gospel without discovering gratitude in my heart. God has done everything for me; He has given me the opportunity of a lifetime. Why wouldn't I want to sacrifice my time and energy to the Lord? Paul considered this fact on multiple occasions in his writings. Let's examine a couple of them:

Titus 2:11-14
For the grace of God has appeared, bringing salvation for all people, training us to renounce ungodliness and worldly passions, and to live self-controlled, upright, and godly lives in the present age, waiting for our blessed hope, the appearing of the glory of our great God and Savior Jesus Christ, who gave himself for us to redeem us from all lawlessness and to purify for himself a people for his own possession who are zealous for good works.

The grace of God is meant to work upon our hearts. Not only does grace bring about salvation, it should produce gratitude in us. Gratitude which should quickly turn into action.

Whenever parents get older and more feeble, it is the responsibility of their kids to care for them. Generally, that is no issue at all because of everything the parents have already done for their kids. Children, out of gratitude, will care for their aging parents. Parents give their children love, shelter, and the tools to succeed. The least their children could do is care for them when they are weak.

God has done so much for us and we should give Him credit for that. His goodness should produce discipline because of our thankfulness. Paul even wrote that He redeemed us so that we would be zealous for good works. Discipline and self-control for the sake of godliness are good works. God desires that we pursue holiness and righteousness. A component of holiness is a choice to live differently than the rest of the world. Following through on the choice to be different will take a large measure of self-control. When you are weak and you want to give up, remember the grace you have been given. Jesus instituted the Lord's Supper so that we would constantly have a reminder of his sacrifice for us.

Selected from Ephesians 2:1-10
And you were dead in the trespasses and sins...and were by nature children of wrath, like the rest of mankind. But God, being rich in mercy, because of the great love with which he loved us...made us alive together with Christ—by grace you have been saved...For we are his workmanship, created in Christ Jesus for good works, which God prepared beforehand, that we should walk in them.

Our desire should be for good works, because of the transformation that has come about through Christ. We were without hope, until God's plan of salvation was completed. God has turned us, His people, into His masterpieces. We are remade into someone who is pleasing to God. We are created with a purpose in mind—good works. God's plan for mankind's salvation does not end in the waters of baptism. Instead, that is the beginning. Forgiveness is the point where God remade us, and gave us new life. From there, we are involved in service to God. Our service will take many shapes and sizes, among which is our discipline toward godliness.

All of this flows from our gratitude toward God. The first 3 verses of Ephesians 2 are among the most depressing in all of Scripture. The next 7 (vs. 4-10) are among the most encouraging. Paul is famous for his 'but' statements and this one ranks toward the top. In spite of our wickedness, God's mercy and love shine forth. We did nothing to deserve what God did for us. The least we can do is live a life of service to Him.

The early Christians set forth an example for discipline that we have to follow. They disciplined themselves to be ready for the difficulties that awaited them, to reconnect with God, or as an act of gratitude for what the Lord had done for them. Their pattern gives us direction for self-control and discipline in our lives today.

Christ

At the close of this chapter, I want to focus our attention back on Jesus. We look to him as an example and we follow his teachings as closely as possible. Among those is the commitment to following him daily.

Luke 9:23
And he said to all, "If anyone would come after me, let him deny himself
and take up his cross daily and follow me.

Following Jesus is a daily commitment to self-denial. The sum total of our service to God is patterning our life after Christ's. Paul later said, *"It is no longer I who live, but Christ who lives in me" (Galatians 2:20)*. The pursuit of living like Jesus will involve repetition. We need to deny ourselves every day.

What did people do when they carried crosses in that day? They were crucified on them. Our self-denial culminates in our own crucifixion. Paul said in Galatians 2 that we are crucified with Christ. Our lives should be about the Father's business like Jesus' was. We are giving our lives over to be used by God. We will need to exercise consistent humility in order that God's will is done, above our own. There may be things that we have to give up, if they are not compatible with the life of a Christian, but it is a path worth taking. The discipline that God expects from us is well worth the suffering.

We have the goal of being with God through eternity and He has made the way possible. If you need one more ounce of motivation, I'm about to give a truck load.

Philippians 3:12-14
Not that I have already obtained this or am already perfect, but I press on to make it my own, because Christ Jesus has made me his own. Brothers, I do not consider that I have made it my own. But one thing I do: forgetting what lies behind and straining forward to what lies ahead, I press on toward the goal for the prize of the upward call of God in Christ Jesus.

We are pressing on toward the goal for the prize of the upward call of God in Christ Jesus. Paul felt as though he had not arrived yet. He understood that as long as he had life, he had more work to do. He forgot everything that held him back and he pressed on for one major reason—because Christ Jesus made him his own.

Why do you have to read? Why do you have to pray? Why do you have to suffer for the cause of Christ? Why do you have to exercise your faith? Because Christ Jesus made you his own. Christ left the throne room, was hated, suffered, bled, and died so that you can have the opportunity to follow him. What more motivation do we need? We aim to make him our own because he made us his own. He valued us enough to sacrifice for us. Our responsibility is to act in gratitude, by repetitively following him. It will not be easy and there will need to be discipline in our hearts, but it is what he deserves. Christ deserves my best. Christ deserves my habits and my heart. God deserves it all because He has given it all to me.

Chapter 8

Conviction

"It's the repetition of affirmations that leads to belief. And once that belief becomes a deep conviction, things begin to happen." —Muhammad Ali

Have you ever felt empty? I've known people that were incredibly successful in their careers, but they felt unfulfilled. They were looking for something, but really didn't quite know what they were supposed to be looking for. When we look for value in our jobs, money, or other physical things, we will come up empty. There is a certain hollowness in the physical things we desire that we don't initially see. God has placed longings within us that the things of this life cannot satisfy.

God confronted His people through the prophet Jeremiah about this very issue, *"For my people have committed two evils: they have forsaken me, the fountain of living waters, and hewed out cisterns for themselves, broken cisterns that can hold no water" (Jeremiah 2:13).* They looked to other gods to satisfy their needs, in much the same way we might look to our careers or money to find satisfaction. God, who is the fountain of living waters, wants us to find our joy in Him. When we look to anything other than God to give us happiness, our cisterns are full of holes. We are no longer able to be filled. The problem is not about how successful we are; the problem lies in what we are seeking. God wants us to find our joy in Him. He is the only one that is able to take us and make us into a vessel for His glory.

We discover true joy, and often happiness, when we are convicted of the immense love of God for us in Christ. His love is deeper than the depths of the oceans, and wider than the galaxies. When we have our convictions deeply rooted in Christ, we will find what we have always been looking for. He will continually fill us with living water.

Conviction

What is conviction? More often than not, it is a word reserved for judicial proceedings. We use the word conviction to speak about how someone was accused of something, the evidence supports that accusation, and a governing body has pronounced a judgment. They are convicted, which means they will face the penalty for their actions. Notice how the word is not used to speak of suspicion. Someone is convicted when everyone that has a say in the matter is confident they did it. The Bible also uses the words convict or conviction in this way, but it is not the emphasis of our study.

A conviction is also a belief that is so strong that it changes your actions. We have convictions about every day life. My family cares deeply about our personal health. Due to the conviction that personal health is important for everyday life, my wife and I exercise at least a few times a week and try to eat healthy foods. Our belief changes our daily actions.

As a society, we are convicted that education is important—which it is. We teach our young people to value school. We help them put in the work to learn what they need to know to contribute to society. Our government does what it can to help our education system be as good as it can be. A conviction changes people's actions.

For a long time, no one knew about the negative effects of smoking; it was a popular thing to do. However, when the health effects became known, it declined in popularity. It became abundantly clear that your health is in danger if you habitually smoke. People try their best to quit, because they know how bad it is for their health. When people knew, they acted differently.

The problem with multitudes of Christians is they lack conviction. If more Christians were convicted of Christ's love, they would try to show it to the world. A general lack of action among Christians can be attributed to a lack of conviction. Anything we *actually* believe causes us to make a lifestyle change. If we really believed our neighbor was headed to Hell apart from Christ, wouldn't we talk to him? If we actually believed the wages of sin was death, would we continue to live as a slave to it? If we truly believe in the power of God in the Church, how can we lack faith? Jesus knew that convictions produced actions, which is why he said that you would know a tree by its fruits. Muhammad Ali hit the nail on the head when he said, *"It's the repetition of affirmations that leads to belief. And once that belief becomes a deep conviction, things begin to happen."* His convictions caused him to be the elite athlete that he was. Our convictions drive us into action.

Convicted

When I think of conviction, 2 Timothy 1:12 comes to mind, which reads *"Which is why I suffer as I do. But I am not ashamed, for I know whom I have believed, and I am convinced that He is able to guard until that Day what has been entrusted to me."* When I let that passage marinate, I can't help but notice how confident Paul was. He was willing to suffer imprisonment, beatings, and persecution for something he believed. Mere belief isn't even the full picture. It was not wishful thinking or a blind belief in something. It was a belief that bordered on knowledge; it was conviction. The ESV used the word "convinced," but "persuaded" is also an accurate rendering. Paul was so convinced in the power of God, he was willing to rest his life on it. He didn't wake up one day with that level of commitment. The Lord worked upon his heart during a span of years. God had worked in Paul's life in such a way that he knew it had to be God's handiwork. I dare say if you look back on your life, you can see His hand. God has been working on you for years.

We are still benefitting from the testimonies of people who walked with Jesus. There were hundreds who saw the resurrected Christ, who shared their experiences in the New Testament. We learn from their level of commitment. One of the most telling proofs of the importance of Jesus is the fact that almost all of the Apostles died for their convictions. They could have claimed that Jesus was a fraud, but not a single one did. Like Paul, they were persuaded that Jesus was/is the Son of God. He deserves our praise!

We should strive for the level of faith that the early Christian leaders had. We have the proof they had, plus the steadfast faithfulness of God for the last two millennia. All who claim the name of Christ should desire to say, with Paul, we *'know whom we have believed and we are convinced that He is able to guard us until that Day.'* God's preservation is far more significant than physical safety. His blessings are literally without end.

How Are We Convicted?

The night before Jesus died on the cross he had an intimate gathering with the twelve apostles. During that time he told them some of the events that were about to take place, one of which being the sending of the Holy Spirit. Jesus told the apostles about how the Spirit would convict the world of their guilt before God (John 16:5-11). This conviction is in the judicial sense—where we understand, through the Holy Spirit, that our sin separates us from God.

In addition to judicial conviction, the Holy Spirit will lead the Apostles into all truth (John 16:13). Truth is the only legitimate foundation for belief, faith, and conviction. The Holy Spirit, by leading us into all truth, is the way in which God imparts faith/conviction to us. God's Spirit led the Apostles to write what they wrote, which is what guides our obedience to this very day. The Holy Spirit is vital to our convictions in the Almighty God. Not only did the Spirit lead the Apostles in all truth, the Spirit dwells within Christians today (1 Corinthians 3:16 & 1 Corinthians 6:19)! We are vessels of the Holy Spirit. If you are in Christ, you have the Spirit. The way in which you gain conviction is through the guiding of the Holy Spirit. God's Spirit works in our lives through the Word of God, and in other ways in which we cannot express (Romans 8). Praise be to God for the working of the Holy Spirit upon our hearts!

The Final Word

We have seen the power of God. God continues to do great things through His people, and His Spirit is aiding us in our service to Him. We desire to continue to learn about God and from Him.

We want to know more of His love for all of creation. Through awe, commitment, love, faith, and discipline, we will grow and want to grow. We can't help but want to serve God. It becomes an obligation we enjoy. God has changed our attitudes and hearts. We have found conviction in the cross.

We will not develop into the Christians God wants us to be until we have conviction in who God is, how much He has done for us, and how much He loves us. For some, who have childlike faith, it takes a short time. For the rest of us, it takes a little while. The gap between committed Christians and superficial ones is conviction. The committed ones have conviction and the nominal ones do not. Don't be discouraged though, God is not done with you yet. Pray for His help on your journey. We need the power of God to transform our lives. Throughout this book, I hope you have learned more about what God has done for you. He wants you to be His child. Continue to commit yourself to His power, learning from Him, and displaying His love to the world.

As we are finding conviction in the Cross, we have an opportunity to meet God anew. We see His grace with fresh eyes. We see the depth and greatness of His gift. I would argue though, that this endeavor lasts our lifetime. We grow in the knowledge of our sin, which increases our understanding of His grace.

In the meantime, His grace through Christ propels us forward. We no longer drift to and fro. We have divine purpose that lacks no supply. God's greatness and might is by our side. We can accomplish His will on earth. We can show Christ to the world, which is our highest calling. It is our highest charge, because the sacrifice of Christ brings honor and glory to God the Father. It should be a perpetual cycle. As R. C. Sproul put it in *The Holiness of God*, "*From brokenness to mission is the human pattern.*"[1] Our brokenness forces us to be in awe of God's mercy, to heal sinners like us. God commissions us to share His message with the nations. We are to lead others to find meaning and purpose in Him. We point them to the Cross of Christ. There they can also find the love of God, that changes the hearts of the most vile individuals.

Jesus should be at the center of our message. Charles Spurgeon said, *"Whatever subject I preach, I do not stop until I reach the Savior, the Lord Jesus, for in Him are all things."* The message of Jesus and his crucifixion should be held close to our hearts. When we observe what he did for us, we do not lack conviction. We look back with teary eyes on that day at Calvary that should spark a lifetime of devotion to Him. We have received favor we never deserved in the form of Jesus, God's only begotten Son, and in him we find conviction in the cross.

Notes

Citation, and use in this book, does not imply author endorses everything believed or taught by cited authors.

Chapter 1-Power

[1]Houston, Brian. *There Is More: When the World Says You Cant, God Says You Can*. Waterbrook PR, 2018.

[2]Lewis, C. S. C. S. *Lewis Classic Collection: Mere Christianity*. Harper One, 2009.

[3]Chan, Francis. *Letters to the Church*. David C. Cook, 2018.

[4] Stein, Robert H. *"Fatherhood of God - Baker's Evangelical Dictionary of Biblical Theology Online."* Bible Study Tools, www.biblestudytools.com/dictionaries/bakers-evangelical-dictionary/fatherhood-of-god.html.

[5]*"'Ask Not What Your Country Can Do for You...".*" *JFK Library*, www.jfklibrary.org/learn/education/teachers/curricular-resources/elementary-school-curricular-resources/ask-not-what-your-country-can-do-for-you.

[6]*"Stress at Work – See Whos Feeling It the Most And How to Overcome It." LinkedIn Learning*, learning.linkedin.com/blog/working-together/stress-at-work-_-see-whos-feeling-it-the-most.

Chapter 2-Learn

[1]Chamorro-Premuzic, Tomas. *"Is Technology Making Us Stupid (and Smarter)?"* Psychology Today, Sussex Publishers, www.psychologytoday.com/us/blog/mr-personality/201305/is-technology-making-us-stupid-and-smarter.

[2]Wilkins, Michael J. *"Disciple, Discipleship - Baker's Evangelical Dictionary of Biblical Theology Online."* Bible Study Tools, www.biblestudytools.com/dictionaries/bakers-evangelical-dictionary/disciple-discipleship.html.

[3]Bauer, Walter, and Frederick W. Danker. *A Greek-English Lexicon of the New Testament and Other Early Christian Literature.* Univ. of Chicago Press, 2000.

[4]Butt, Kyle, and Eric Lyons. *Reasons To Believe.* Apologetics Press, Inc., 2017.

[5]Strong's Greek: 365. *Ἀνανεόω (Ananeoó) -- to Renew,* biblehub.com/greek/365.htm.

[6]Tozer, A. W. *The Pursuit of God.* Christian Publications, 1948.

[7]Whitney, Donald S. *Spiritual Disciplines for the Christian Life.* NavPress, 2014.

[8]*"State of the Bible 2017: Top Findings."* Barna Group, www.barna.com/research/state-bible-2017-top-findings/.

Chapter 3-Love

[1]Endsley, Courtney. *"How the Transcontinental Railroad Changed America."* GTG Technology Group, 4 Nov. 2016, gtgtechnologygroup.com/transcontinental-railroad/.

[2]Manning, Brennan. *The Ragamuffin Gospel: Good News for the Bedraggled, Beat-up, and Burnt Out.* Multnomah, 1990.

[3]Davies, Godfrey, and Arthur Wellesley. *Duke of. Wellington. Wellington and His Army.* Greenwood, 1974.

[4]Keller, Timothy. *The Prodigal God: Recovering the Heart of the Christian Faith.* Penguin Books, 2016.

[5]Tozer, A. W., and James L. Snyder. *The Crucified Life.* Regal/From Gospel Light, 2011.

[6]Kittel, Gerhard, and Ethelbert Stauffer. *Theological Dictionary of the New Testament, Vol. 1-10.* Eerdman, 1964.

[7]Robertson, Archibald Thomas. *Word Pictures in the New Testament: Volume 4 - The Epistles of Paul.* Baker Book House, 1930.

Chapter 4-Faith

[1]Moreland, James Porter. *Love Your God with All Your Mind the Role of Reason in the Life of the Soul.* The Navigators, 2014.

2*"George Muller."* George Muller - New World Encyclopedia, www.newworldencyclopedia.org/entry/George_Muller.

3Biography.com Editors. *"Corrie Ten Boom."* Biography.com, A&E Networks Television, 17 Apr. 2019, www.biography.com/people/corrie-ten-boom-21358155#world-war-ii-changes-everything).

4North, Ira. *Balance: A Tried & Tested Formula for Church Growth.* Gospel Advocate Co., 1983.

Chapter 5-Worship

1Tozer, A. W., and James L. Snyder. *The Purpose of Man: Designed to Worship.* Bethany House, 2014.

2Keller, Timothy. *The Reason for God: Belief in an Age of Scepticism.* Hodder & Stoughton, 2009.

3Tozer, A. W., and James L. Snyder. *The Purpose of Man: Designed to Worship.* Bethany House, 2014.

4Bauer, Walter, and Frederick W. Danker. *A Greek-English Lexicon of the New Testament and Other Early Christian Literature.* Univ. of Chicago Press, 2000.

5Schwartz, David Joseph. *The Magic of Thinking Big.* A. Thomas and Company, 1967.

6Tozer, A. W., and James L. Snyder. *The Purpose of Man: Designed to Worship.* Bethany House, 2014.

Chapter 6-Fellowship

[1]Bauer, Walter, and Frederick W. Danker. *A Greek-English Lexicon of the New Testament and Other Early Christian Literature.* Univ. of Chicago Press, 2000.

[2]Kittel, Gerhard, and Friedrich Hauck. *Theological Dictionary of the New Testament, Vol. 1-10.* Eerdman, 1964.

[3]Packer, J. I. *Knowing God.* Hodder & Stoughton, 2013.

[4]Tozer, A. W. *The Knowledge of the Holy.* HarperOne, 1978.

[5]Thumma, Scott, and Warren Bird. *The Other Eighty Percent: Turning Your Churchs Spectators into Active Disciples.* Jossey-Bass, 2011.

[6]Lewis, C. S. *C. S. Lewis Classic Collection: Mere Christianity.* Harper One, 2009.

[7]Packer, J. I. *Knowing God.* Hodder & Stoughton, 2013.

Chapter 7-Repeat

[1]Whitney, Donald S. *Spiritual Disciplines for the Christian Life.* NavPress, 2014.

[2]Rugnetta, Michael. "Neuroplasticity." *Encyclopædia Britannica,* Encyclopædia Britannica, Inc., www.britannica.com/science/neuroplasticity.

Finding Conviction in the Cross

[3]"Infographic: You Have More Time for Bible Reading than You Think." *Crossway Articles*, www.crossway.org/articles/infographic-you-can-read-more-of-the-bible-than-you-think/.

[4]Hyatt, Michael. *Your Best Year Ever a 5-Step Plan for Achieving Your Most Important Goals*. Baker Books, a Division of Baker Publishing Group, 2018.

[5]Gladwell, Malcolm. *Outliers: the Story of Success*. Back Bay Books, 2013.

Chapter 8-Conviction

[1]Sproul, R. C. *The Holiness of God*. Tyndale House Publishers, 1998.

Acknowledgements

A big thank you goes out to the editing team. Their counsel was invaluable in creating the final product you now hold. Each of these individuals holds a special place in my heart.

Allen Barker

Andy Brewster

Clinton Rowand

Dakota Moody

Jessi Spring

Shannon O'Bryan

Skip Wilson

Now, I've saved the best for last. Thank you, MacKenzie. Your support and editing are a big reason why I was able to finish this book. I love you.

Thank you for reading *Finding Conviction In The Cross*.
I pray that it has been a blessing to your life.

Please share this book with anyone you know who
would benefit from it.

To learn more about *Finding Conviction In The Cross*
check out findingconvictioninthecross.com

More copies of this book can be purchased on
amazon.com or by contacting me at
michaelrowand@yahoo.com

For any spiritual concerns that I may be able to help
with, contact me at michaelrowand@yahoo.com.